The
Ultimate
Frozen
Dessert
Book

A Complete Guide to Gelato, Sherbet, Granita, and Semifreddo, Plus Frozen Cakes, Pies, Mousses, Chiffon Cakes, and More, with Hundreds of Ways to Customize Every Recipe to Your Own Taste

The Ultimate Frozen Dessert Book

BRUCE WEINSTEIN AND

MARK SCARBROUGH

wm

WILLIAM MORROW

An Imprint of HarperCollinsPublishers

To Jane Friedman. We adore you, too.

Our melting thanks to

KitchenAid for a PRO LINE Frozen Dessert Maker; Kim Roman, our Saatchi Santa; Brian Maynard at KitchenAid, our appliance amigo; Harriet Bell, our fabulous editor; Lucy Baker, our forgiving timekeeper and mistake-eraser; Susan Ginsburg, our first-rate agent; Rachel Specter, our now lamentably gone enabler; Emily Saladino, learning the enabler's art; Beth Shepard, our media mogul; Pat Adrian, a constant friend; Diane Aronson, a production genius; Leah Carlson-Stanisic, Jessica Peskay, and Karen Lumley, three production graces; Elizabeth Ackerman and Sarah Maya Gubkin, design gurus; Virginia McRae, our top-notch copy editor; Carrie Bachman, Jonathan Schwartz, and Bobbilyn Jones, publicity mavens all; Robert Steinberg, our chocolate cherub

THE ULTIMATE FROZEN DESSERT BOOK. Copyright © 2005 by Bruce Weinstein and Mark Scarbrough. All rights reserved. Printed in the United States of America. No part of this book may be used or reproduced in any manner whatsoever without written permission except in the case of brief quotations embodied in critical articles and reviews. For information address HarperCollins Publishers Inc., 10 East 53rd Street, New York, NY 10022.

HarperCollins books may be purchased for educational, business, or sales promotional use. For information please write: Special Markets Department, HarperCollins Publishers Inc., 10 East 53rd Street, New York, NY 10022.

FIRST EDITION

DESIGNED BY SARAH MAYA GUBKIN

Printed on acid-free paper

Library of Congress Cataloging-in-Publication Data

Weinstein, Bruce, 1960–
    The ultimate frozen dessert book : a complete guide to gelato, sherbet, granita, and semifreddo, plus frozen cakes, pies, mousses, chiffon cakes, and more, with hundreds of ways to customize every recipe to your own taste / Bruce Weinstein and Mark Scarbrough.
        p. cm.
    ISBN 0-06-059707-0
    1. Ice cream, ices, etc.   2. Frozen desserts.   I. Scarbrough, Mark.   II. Title.

TX795.W44 2005
641.8'62—dc22   2004055968

05   06   07   08   09   WBC/QW   10   9   8   7   6   5   4   3   2   1

Contents

Introduction

In this compendium of frozen desserts, you'll find everything from an over-the-top nougat semifreddo to an easy, refreshing raspberry granita, perfect for a hot afternoon. You'll find dozens of gelati with hundreds of ways to customize them, as well as all sorts of frozen cakes, pies, and mousses. But what you won't find are traditional ice creams or sorbets. Those are in a companion volume, *The Ultimate Ice Cream Book,* the book that started our series of Ultimate books: party drinks, candy, shrimp, brownies, potatoes, muffins, and chocolate cookies. Now, in this ninth volume, we've come full circle, back to where it all started: our love affair with cold, sweet treats.

What is it about frozen desserts that makes them so irresistible? Stand in line at an ice cream shop and you feel a camaraderie with those around you. You smile, you wait (patiently or not), you even chitchat with complete strangers. (You certainly don't act like that when you notice someone in a restaurant eating a piece of the same pie you've ordered.) Maybe, for a brief moment, we all revert to being kids waiting for cones. Maybe it's the singular strangeness of eating something cold and creamy—isn't food supposed to be hot from the fire? Or maybe we never really get over the thrill of frozen desserts.

The Ultimate Frozen Dessert Book is divided into five chapters, each covering a different treat:

- **Gelato**, an Italian frozen custard, a favorite of ice cream aficionados. Most adore its velvety texture, a rich mixture of whole milk and egg yolks.
- **Sherbet**, originally a Middle Eastern refresher, made without eggs—just milk, sugar, and a fruit puree. Creamy, yet refreshing, it's perfect for an evening out on the deck.
- **Granita**, an icy treat made without eggs or milk, just sugar and fruit—light, cold, and filled with flavor.
- **Semifreddo**, that most decadent of Italian frozen desserts: a marshmallowy "cake" that's frozen in a loaf pan and cut into slices.
- Frozen **pies, mousses, terrines, and ice cream cakes,** those stunning bring-it-to-the-pot-luck or make-it-ahead-for-the-dinner-party desserts. Many are made with gelati from this book—or with store-bought ice cream.

As in the other Ultimate books, we list the recipes in each chapter alphabetically: Almond Gelato, Anise Gelato, Apricot Gelato, and so on. We use the English name except where the Italian proves untranslatable (Bacio Gelato, for example). After many recipes, we include ways to customize them to your taste: add a splash of extract, a little fresh juice, some dried fruit, or a handful of chocolate chips, and you have a dessert that's utterly your own. In the end, it's all about making what you want—and we all want as many frozen desserts as we can make.

Gelato

Gelato is ice cream without the cream—just whole milk and egg yolks. In fact, it's dense and smooth because of what it doesn't have: cream and egg whites. These readily whip up when beaten; they even turn airy when just stirred repeatedly. Egg yolks? Far less so—unless they're part of a custard base as it begins to freeze in your ice cream machine. As it does, the yolks trap a tiny bit of air between their crowded cell walls—and voilà, the difference: a denser consistency, creamier despite the lack of cream.

What else is missing in gelati (that is, the plural of *gelato*)? Thickeners like flour, cornstarch, or gelatin. They're often necessary in standard ice cream because of the inclusion of those loosy-goosy egg whites and the relatively small ratio of egg yolks to sugar. Gelato, rich in egg-yolk protein, needs no such help.

Gelato begins with an egg custard—a sugary mixture that's cooked until the proteins build a coherent structure among the components. Technically speaking, then, gelato is frozen custard. But it's not necessarily American-style frozen custard, which has plenty of whole eggs, not just the yolks.

More often than not, American-style frozen custard also contains cream. In fact, much of what's sold as gelato in North America has a high cream content, sometimes even higher than standard ice cream. We suspect that's because egg yolks are high-priced and cholesterol-rich. If we were to cut the egg yolks in half in our gelati recipes and replace what's missing with cream, we'd end up with a lower-cholesterol product, but it wouldn't be Italian gelato. It would be some strange hybrid, an ice cream with more egg yolks.

Still and all, the gelati in this book do indeed contain a little cream. Here's why—the whole milk sold in the United States is not as rich as that sold in Italy. Ours has just over 3 percent butterfat, sometimes a smidge more in states like California that legislate a slightly higher fat content. By contrast, Italian whole milk has around 3.7 percent butterfat. That may well be the lowest in the European Union—France's runs around 4.1 percent; Denmark's, more than 4.3 percent—but the difference matters a great deal. So homemade gelato made with U.S. whole milk needs a "fat compensation" for that real Italian taste—thus, the addition of a small amount of cream.

But egg whites and cream are minor concerns when compared with something as seemingly innocuous as air. Gelato is supposed to be dense, exceptionally so. Too much air beaten into the custard must surely be the gravest of culinary indiscretions.

How do you know how much air has gotten into a frozen custard? Simply measure the volume of custard you put into the machine, then measure the volume of gelato that comes out. In professional parlance, the difference is expressed as a percentage increase and called the "overrun" (that is, the amount over and above the original base).

Most commercial ice cream has a 100 percent overrun. It's half air; for each tablespoon of base put into the machine, two tablespoons come out. Premium ice cream has an overrun below 33 percent; super premium, sold strictly in pints, around 20 percent. But gelato has still less—traditionally, under 10 percent, often as little as 2 percent. In other words, if you put 4 cups (1 quart) of custard into your machine, you should end up with no more than 4⅓ cups gelato (about an 8 percent overrun)—although ideally you should end up with just slightly more than 1 quart, maybe even just 1 tablespoon more.

The point is this: you want the least amount of air in the custard. To that end, we have some tips for making authentic gelato every time.

A Dozen Tips for Gelato Success

1. Start with the best ingredients you can comfortably afford. Use high-quality chocolate, fresh eggs and milk, real vanilla and other extracts. If the fruit you buy has no smell, it will probably have no taste.

2. Let the milk and egg yolks sit for 10 minutes at room temperature before you begin. Cold ingredients will slow down the cooking—and thus more air will get into the custard as you stir endlessly, waiting for the mixture to heat up and thicken.

3. If possible, make the custard with a whisk, preferably a balloon whisk. Although you can use an electric mixer, it will definitely get more air into the custard and the resulting gelato will not be as dense as the hand-whisked variety.

4. All these recipes make about 1 quart of gelato. To make a half-gallon for a traditional bucket-churning maker or one of the new frozen dessert machines, double the recipe and adjust the heating times (i.e., add a few minutes for the custard to thicken).

5. As you heat the combined eggs and milk, work over low heat so as not to scramble the eggs; stir constantly to allow for even coagulation. Cook the custard until it coats the back of a wooden spoon—a funny-sounding step, but essential. Stir well with a wooden spoon, then run your finger across its back. The line should be firm—no running liquid or sagging custard at its margins. It all happens relatively quickly, but you can even cook the custard a minute or two longer. The longer you heat the mixture, the eggier it will taste. If you heat the custard until it's foamy, just seconds before the eggs scramble, you'll have very eggy gelato—to some people's taste, but not to others'.

6. Strain the custard through a fine-mesh sieve to remove any unwanted bits of scrambled eggs that inadvertently make their way into the custard. A conical chinoise works best, but you can also line a colander with cheesecloth.

7. Refrigerate the custard before you freeze it, for at least 4 hours, or overnight. Once the warmed custard has cooled, cover the bowl with plastic wrap to protect the mixture from any refrigerator odors.

8. Just before you freeze the custard in your ice cream machine, place it in your freezer for 10 minutes. Shocking the custard with a final chill will safeguard against air getting into the gelato as the machine churns it.

9. Always transfer the frozen gelato from your ice cream machine to a separate container before storing it in your refrigerator's freezer. You can damage your machine's container or its nonstick surface if you try to dig hardened gelato out of it.

10. Gelato tastes best at slightly above its freezing point (which varies dramatically based on the sugars and salt in the custard). When the gelato is soft, the intense flavors and aromas have a chance to volatilize out of icy suspension. The best way to eat gelato is straight out of the machine. If, however, you've stored it in the freezer, always leave it out on the counter for 10 minutes before serving.

11. Refreezing is the surest way to end up with icy gelato. Consider storing gelato in smaller containers, even individual-serving ones.

12. Finally, what's a cook to do with all those leftover egg whites? Place them in an airtight container and freeze for up to 6 months; defrost overnight in the refrigerator and use in egg-white omelets, meringue cookies, or an angel-food cake.

About Mix-Ins

In many of the variations, we offer ways to customize the gelato by your adding some chopped nuts, chocolate chips, or the like, just before the gelato firms up. If you're working with a smaller, countertop machine, let the dasher give the mix-ins a few turns just before the gelato is ready to serve. For old-fashioned canister machines, first take off the motor housing—then either add the mix-ins, remount the motor, and let the machine go a few more turns; or stir in the mix-ins by hand, using the dasher as a large spatula. For frozen dessert machines that dispense gelato through a pull-handle, proceed in one of two ways. Stir the mix-ins into the chilled custard before adding it to the machine, letting the gelato then freeze as directed; to serve, remove the dispenser housing and scoop out the gelato. Or forgo adding the mix-ins until the very end—open the dispenser nozzle and let the gelato fall into a storage container; as it does so, crumble in the additions in a steady, slow stream, layering them into the gelato.

Almond Gelato

Makes about 1 quart (can be doubled for half-gallon machines)

Here's a surprisingly light gelato, perfect for a summer treat on the deck or along-side an autumn apple tart. Almond gelato also makes for one terrific hot fudge sundae—like a cold but soft Almond Joy bar!

> 2¾ cups whole milk
> ¼ cup heavy cream
> One 7-ounce tube almond paste (see Note)
> ⅔ cup sugar
> 5 large egg yolks, at room temperature
> ½ teaspoon almond extract
> ¼ teaspoon salt

1. Heat the milk and cream in a medium saucepan set over medium heat until tiny bubbles fizz around the pan's inner rim. Adjust the heat so the mixture stays this hot but does not come to a boil.

2. Place the almond paste and sugar in a large food processor fitted with the chopping blade; process until the texture of fine sand, about 1 minute. Stop the machine, add the yolks all at once, and process until light and thick, about 2 minutes.

3. With the machine running, dribble in about half of the hot milk mixture through the feed tube; process until smooth. Then whisk this mixture back into the pan with the remaining hot milk mixture. Instantly reduce the heat to very low—if you have electric burners, place the pan on a second one just now set on low. Cook slowly, stirring all the while, until the mixture thickens to the consistency of wet but smooth pancake batter and can coat the back of a wooden spoon, a little less than 2 minutes. Strain through a fine-mesh sieve into a clean bowl to get rid of any extraneous bits of scrambled egg; stir in the almond extract and salt. Refrigerate until cold, for at least 4 hours, or overnight.

4. Just before making the gelato, place the almond custard and your ice cream machine's dasher, if possible, in the freezer to shock them extra cold, for no more than 10 minutes.

5. Freeze the custard in your ice cream machine according to the manufacturer's instructions. Serve at once—or transfer to a large container or several smaller containers, seal tightly, and store in the freezer for up to 1 month; soften at room temperature for up to 10 minutes before serving.

NOTE: Almond paste can be found in the baking aisle of almost every supermarket. The paste should be soft and moist; check by squeezing the tube before buying it.

Almond Candy Bar Gelato   Add ½ cup semisweet chocolate chips and ½ cup sweetened shredded coconut to the machine when the gelato is almost firm, or mix them into the finished gelato as it's placed in a storage container.

Almond Chocolate Swirl   As you transfer the finished gelato to a storage container, take 1 cup chocolate ice cream sauce or spoonable hot fudge sauce and layer it with the gelato in the container—add some gelato, then some chocolate sauce, then some more gelato, etc., creating ribbons of chocolate in the almond gelato.

Almond Honey Gelato   Substitute an equal amount of honey for the sugar.

Almond Nougatine Gelato   Make the almond nougatine for the Torroncino Gelato (page 96), crumble it up when cool, and stir it into the chilled custard before freezing.

Almond Toffee Gelato   Add ⅔ cup crushed toffee candy, such as Heath bar or Skor, to the machine just before the gelato sets, or add it to the finished gelato as it's put into a storage container.

Toasted Almond Gelato   Toast ⅔ cup sliced almonds with 1 tablespoon unsalted butter in a large skillet set over medium heat until very fragrant; cool 10 minutes. Add the almonds to the chilled custard before freezing, or use the almonds as a mix-in to the almost finished gelato in the machine.

Anise Gelato

Makes about 1 quart (can be doubled for half-gallon machines)

We've upped the cream in this classic so its texture is a little lighter—a better foil, we feel, to the spiky taste of anise. Don't substitute fennel seeds—the taste is cloying. Serve this gelato with fresh blackberries for a summertime treat.

> 2½ cups whole milk
> 1 cup heavy cream
> 2 teaspoons anise seeds
> 4 large egg yolks, at room temperature
> ⅔ cup sugar
> ¼ teaspoon salt

1. Heat the milk and cream in a medium saucepan set over medium heat until small bubbles pop up along the pan's inner rim. Stir in the anise seeds, cover the pan, remove from the heat, and steep for 15 minutes.

2. Meanwhile, beat the egg yolks and sugar in a medium bowl with a whisk or an electric mixer at medium speed until thick and pale yellow, almost beige, even if still a little grainy from the sugar, about 2 minutes.

3. Whisk about a third of the hot milk mixture into this egg-yolk mixture until smooth, then whisk the combined mixture back into the remaining warm milk mixture in the pan. Set over very low heat and cook, stirring constantly, until the mixture begins to get foamy, rises up in the pan, and can coat the back of a wooden spoon, about 6 minutes. Strain through a fine-mesh sieve into a second, clean bowl to remove the anise seeds; stir in the salt. Refrigerate until cold, for about 4 hours, or overnight.

4. While you prepare your ice cream machine, place the anise custard and your machine's dasher, if possible, in the freezer to assure they're very cold, for no more than 10 minutes.

5. Freeze the custard in your ice cream machine according to the manufacturer's instructions. Serve at once—or scoop it into a large container or several smaller containers, seal well, and store in the freezer for up to 1 month; soften at room temperature for up to 10 minutes before serving.

Customize it!
Add ½ cup of any of the following, or any combination of the following, to the machine when the gelato is almost set, or stir into the finished gelato as it goes into a storage container: candied lemon rind, candied orange rind, chopped amaretti, chopped biscotti, chopped dried pears, chopped Good & Plenty candies, chopped pistachios, dried cherries, dried strawberries, or mini chocolate chips.

Apricot Gelato

Makes about 1 quart (can be doubled for half-gallon machines)

Because apricots are in season for just a few weeks, we suggest the concentrated flavor of dried apricots for a year-round treat. Rather than dried Turkish apricots, buy California apricot halves—darker in color and quite tart.

> 5 ounces dried California apricot halves (about 1¼ cups,
>   see Note)
> One 11½-ounce can apricot nectar
> 2 cups whole milk
> ½ cup heavy cream
> 5 large egg yolks, at room temperature
> 1 cup sugar
> 1 teaspoon vanilla extract
> ¼ teaspoon salt

1. Place the dried apricots in a medium bowl and set aside. Bring the apricot nectar to a simmer in a small saucepan set over medium-high heat. Pour the hot nectar over the dried apricots and soak at room temperature, stirring once in a while, until softened, about 1 hour.

2. Drain the softened apricot halves, reserving ¼ cup of the soaking liquid. Place the apricots and the reserved liquid in a blender or a large food processor fitted with the chopping blade; blend or process until fairly smooth.

3. Pour the puree into a fine-mesh sieve set over a medium bowl; gently push the puree through the mesh with the back of a wooden spoon to strain out any flecks of skin. (Alternatively, you can put the puree through a food mill set over a medium bowl.) Set this strained puree aside. (The recipe can be made up to this point 2 days in advance; store the strained puree, tightly covered, in the refrigerator—let it come to room temperature before proceeding.)

4. Heat the milk and cream in a medium saucepan set over medium heat, just until small bubbles line the pan's inside rim. Do not boil.

5. Beat the egg yolks and sugar with a whisk or an electric mixer at medium speed, until pale yellow, thick, and gooey-grainy, about 2 minutes. Whisk about a third of the hot milk mixture into this egg-yolk mixture until smooth, then whisk this combined mixture back into the remaining hot milk mixture. Immediately reduce the heat to very low—if you're using an electric stove, move the pan to an unused burner set on low. Cook slowly, stirring constantly, until the mixture thickens to the consistency of wet, smooth pancake batter and can coat the back of a wooden spoon, about 4 minutes. Strain through a clean fine-mesh sieve into a second bowl; stir in the apricot puree, vanilla, and salt. Refrigerate until cold, for at least 4 hours, or overnight.

6. As you prepare your ice cream machine, place the chilled custard and the machine's dasher, if possible, in the freezer to make sure they're cold, for no more than 10 minutes.

7. Freeze the custard in your ice cream machine according to the manufacturer's instructions. Serve at once—or transfer to a large container or several smaller containers, seal tightly, and store in your freezer for up to 1 month; soften at room temperature for up to 10 minutes before serving.

NOTE: Sulphured apricots have been doped with sulphur dioxide to keep their color brighter. It makes for prettier gelato, but you can use unsulphured dried apricots if you want to forgo the chemical doping and don't mind a dark brown gelato.

Apricot Coffee Cake Gelato   Add 1 cup chopped purchased coffee cake (½-inch cubes) and ¼ cup chopped walnuts to the machine just before the gelato sets, or stir them into the finished gelato as it goes into a storage container.

Apricot Granola Gelato   Stir 1 cup purchased granola into the machine just before the gelato sets, or into the finished gelato as it's put in a storage container.

Apricot Honey Gelato   Reduce the sugar to ½ cup and add ½ cup honey with the remaining sugar.

Apricot Maple Gelato   Substitute maple sugar for the sugar.

Apricot Strawberry Gelato   Drizzle purchased strawberry ice cream sauce into the finished gelato as it goes into a storage container, making ribbons of strawberry sauce between layers of gelato.

Mendiant Gelato   Add ⅓ cup mini chocolate chips and ⅓ cup chopped pistachios to the machine just before the gelato sets. Stir them into the finished gelato as it's put in a storage container.

Nutty Apricot Gelato   Add ⅔ cup chopped hazelnuts, pecans, or walnuts to the chilled custard before it's frozen in the machine, or to the machine just before the gelato sets.

Bacio Gelato

Makes about 1 quart (can be doubled for half-gallon machines)

There's no adequate translation for this classic Italian combination of hazelnuts and dark chocolate—other than to say it's delicious. Recipes like this one that ask you to steep nuts in whole milk call for cheesecloth to line a sieve or colander. You can find cheesecloth at some high-end supermarkets, almost all baking supply stores, and outlets listed in the Source Guide (page 241).

> ¾ **cup whole hazelnuts**
> 3 **cups whole milk, or more as necessary**
> ¼ **cup heavy cream**
> 2 **ounces unsweetened chocolate, chopped**
> ¾ **cup sugar**
> 3 **large egg yolks, at room temperature**
> ½ **teaspoon vanilla extract**
> ¼ **teaspoon salt**

1. Position a rack in the center of the oven and preheat the oven to 350°F. Spread the hazelnuts out on a large baking sheet and toast in the oven, stirring often, until lightly browned but very fragrant, about 6 minutes.

2. Place the toasted hazelnuts and the milk in a large saucepan, set it over medium heat, and bring the mixture to a low simmer. Adjust the heat so the mixture does not roil up; simmer very slowly for 5 minutes. Cover the pan, remove it from the heat, and steep for 20 minutes. Meanwhile, line a sieve or colander with cheesecloth and set it over a large bowl.

3. Transfer the milk and nuts to a large food processor fitted with the chopping blade or a wide-canister blender. Process or blend until fairly smooth, scraping down the sides of the bowl as necessary (see Note). Transfer the puree to the prepared sieve; drain until almost all the liquid has leached into the bowl, about 15 minutes.

4. Gather the cheesecloth into a ball with the hazelnuts still inside it and hold the cheesecloth over the sieve and the bowl. Squeeze to extract as much milk as possible. You should have about 2½ cups hazelnut milk; if not, add whole milk until the mixture comes up to the required amount. Discard the nuts.

5. Heat the hazelnut milk and cream in a medium saucepan set over medium heat until little bubbles pop up around the pan's inner rim. Remove the pan from the heat, add in the chopped chocolate and ½ cup of the sugar, and stir until smooth. Set aside.

6. Beat the egg yolks and the remaining ¼ cup sugar in a medium bowl with a whisk or an electric mixer at medium speed until thick and light but still grainy, about 2 minutes. Whisk about a quarter of the chocolate mixture into this egg-yolk mixture until smooth, then whisk this combined mixture back into the remaining chocolate mixture in the pan. Set the pan over very low heat and cook, stirring constantly, until a few puffs of steam appear off the surface (no bubbles really) and the mixture is the consistency of melted ice cream, no more than 1 minute. Strain through a fine-mesh sieve into a clean bowl; stir in the vanilla and salt. Refrigerate until cold, for about 4 hours, or overnight.

7. Before you make the gelato, place the custard and your ice cream machine's dasher, if possible, in the freezer just to get them cold, for no more than 10 minutes.

8. Freeze the custard in your ice cream machine according to the manufacturer's instructions. Serve at once—or scoop into a large container or several small ones, even individual-serving-size containers; seal well, and store in the freezer for up to 1 month; soften at room temperature for up to 10 minutes before serving.

NOTE: Hot liquids can spew up in a blender, especially when the lid is on. To prevent this, take off the center cap in the lid, then affix the lid. Cover the open hole loosely with a clean kitchen towel, hold the lid down, and blend until smooth. A little of the hot mixture will roil up, but the hole will allow air to escape as the mixture rises, so it will not spew out the sides of the lid.

Gianduja Gelato   Substitute milk chocolate for the unsweetened chocolate.

White Chocolate Hazelnut Gelato   Substitute white chocolate for the unsweetened chocolate.

Customize it!
Or add ½ teaspoon of any of the following with the vanilla to any of these gelati: almond extract, maple extract, or rum extract

Or add ⅔ cup of any of the following to the machine just before the gelato sets, or stir ⅔ cup into the finished gelato as it's placed into a storage container: chopped dried bananas, chopped dried figs, chopped pitted dates (preferably a soft variety like Medjool), crumbled biscotti, crumbled gingersnaps, crumbled sugar wafers, dried raspberries, golden raisins, mini chocolate chips, peanut butter chips, sweetened shredded coconut, or white chocolate chips.

Banana Gelato

Makes about 1 quart (can be doubled for half-gallon machines)

For the best taste in this velvety gelato, use ripe but still firm bananas, ones with quite a few brown spots on their skins. They should be just a tad past the point where you'd slice them onto cereal.

> **2 very ripe bananas, chopped**
> **1½ cups whole milk**
> **½ cup heavy cream**
> **4 large egg yolks, at room temperature**
> **⅔ cup sugar**
> **1 teaspoon vanilla extract**
> **¼ teaspoon salt**

1. Slowly cook the bananas, milk, and cream in a medium saucepan set over low heat for 10 minutes, stirring constantly. Do not allow the mixture to come to a boil, although the milk may become quite foamy. Transfer to a blender or a large food processor fitted with the chopping blade; blend or process until smooth (see page 16 for a note on how to deal with hot liquids in a blender). Set aside.

2. Beat the egg yolks and sugar with a whisk or an electric mixer at medium speed until thick and somewhat creamy, even if a little grainy, about 2 minutes. Whisk about a third of the warm banana mixture into this egg-yolk mixture, then whisk this combined mixture with the remainder of the hot banana mixture into a medium saucepan. Place over low heat and cook slowly, stirring constantly, until the mixture gets slightly foamy, begins to smell eggy, and can coat the back of a wooden spoon, about 2 minutes. Strain through a fine-mesh sieve into a clean bowl to remove any extraneous bits of scrambled egg; stir in the vanilla and salt. Refrigerate until cold, for about 4 hours, or overnight.

3. As you prepare your ice cream machine, place the banana custard and your machine's dasher, if possible, in the freezer to assure they're very cold, for no more than 10 minutes.

4. Freeze the custard in your ice cream machine according to the manufacturer's instructions. Serve at once—or transfer into a large container or several smaller ones, seal well, and store in the freezer for up to 1 month; soften at room temperature for up to 10 minutes before serving.

Banana Butter Crunch Gelato Add ⅔ cup crushed butter crunch candy to the machine just before the gelato sets or to the finished gelato as it's put in a storage container.

Banana Nut Fudge Gelato Add ½ cup chopped walnuts to the machine just before the gelato sets or to the finished gelato; layer 1 cup purchased hot fudge sauce as the finished gelato's placed in the storage container.

Banana Pineapple Orange Gelato Reduce the milk to 1 cup; add ½ cup orange juice concentrate, thawed, with the vanilla. Add ½ cup chopped dried pineapple to the machine just before the gelato sets or to the finished gelato.

Banana Pudding Gelato Add ½ cup crushed vanilla wafer cookies and ½ cup mini marshmallows to the machine just before the gelato sets or to the finished gelato.

Banana Rocky Road Gelato Add ⅓ cup mini marshmallows, ⅓ cup chopped almonds, and ⅓ cup mini chocolate chips to the machine just before the gelato sets or to the finished gelato.

Banana White Chocolate Macadamia Nut Gelato Add ⅓ cup white chocolate chips and ⅓ cup chopped unsalted macadamia nuts to the machine just before the gelato sets or to the finished gelato.

PB&J Banana Gelato Add ½ cup peanut butter chips to the machine just before the gelato sets or stir into the finished gelato; layer 1 cup strawberry ice cream sauce into the gelato as it's scooped or dispensed into the storage container.

BLACKBERRY GELATO

Makes about 1 quart (can be doubled for half-gallon machines)

Blackberries are perfect for gelato: tart, summery, and intense. Frozen ones are fine, provided they are high-quality, whole berries.

> 2 cups fresh blackberries (1 pint), or one 10-ounce package frozen
>   blackberries, thawed
> 5 large egg yolks, at room temperature
> ¾ cup sugar
> 2 cups whole milk
> ½ cup heavy cream
> ¼ teaspoon salt

1. Place the blackberries in a fine-mesh sieve set over a medium bowl and press them through the mesh with the back of a wooden spoon, scraping the pulp gently across the mesh to extract as much juice and solids as you can while leaving the seeds and skin behind. Set the strained puree aside but do not discard the seeds in the strainer. You should end up with about 1¼ cups blackberry puree.

2. Beat the egg yolks and sugar in a medium bowl with a whisk or an electric mixer at medium speed until pale yellow and thick, like a grainy paste, about 2 minutes.

3. Heat the milk and cream in a medium saucepan set over medium heat until small bubbles dot the pan's inside rim; do not boil but adjust the heat to keep the mixture this hot.

4. Whisk about a third of the hot milk mixture into this egg-yolk mixture until smooth, then whisk this combined mixture into the remaining hot milk mixture until smooth. Immediately reduce the heat to very low—if you're using an electric stove, move the pan to an unused burner just now set on low. Cook slowly, stirring constantly, until the mixture rises slightly in the pan and is thick enough to coat the back of a wooden spoon, about 3 minutes.

5. Add a small amount of the custard to the sieve with the blackberry seeds, and push them again against the mesh into the bowl with the blackberry puree, thereby getting the last amount of pulp out of the seeds. Discard the seeds and wash the strainer. Strain the remaining custard into the bowl with the puree. Add the salt and stir well. Refrigerate until cold, for at least 4 hours, or overnight.

6. As you prepare your ice cream machine, place the custard and the machine's dasher, if possible, in the freezer, just to assure they're cold, for no more than 10 minutes.

7. Freeze the custard in your ice cream machine according to the manufacturer's instructions. Serve at once—or transfer to a large container or many smaller containers, seal tightly, and store in the freezer for up to 1 month; soften at room temperature for up to 10 minutes before serving.

Customize it!
Mix in ½ teaspoon of any of the following with the salt: lemon extract, maple extract, or rum extract

And/or stir ⅓ cup finely chopped crystallized ginger into the chilled custard before it's frozen.

And/or mix ⅔ cup of any of the following, or any combination of the following, into the machine just before the gelato sets or into the finished gelato as it's put in a storage container: chopped pecans, chopped unsalted cashews, chopped unsalted peanuts, crumbled chocolate fudge cookies, crumbled vanilla wafer cookies, or mini marshmallows.

BLUEBERRY GELATO

Makes about 1 quart (can be doubled for half-gallon machines)

Although fresh blueberries are at the peak of flavor in the summer heat, always smell the container to make sure the berries are the most fragrant you can find. Frozen blueberries simply don't have enough punch for this creamy gelato.

> 1½ cups fresh blueberries (about ¾ pint)
> 1 tablespoon lemon juice
> 2 cups whole milk
> ¼ cup heavy cream
> 4 large egg yolks, at room temperature
> ¾ cup sugar
> ½ teaspoon vanilla extract
> ¼ teaspoon salt

1. Place the berries and the lemon juice in a blender or a food processor fitted with the chopping blade; blend or process until fairly smooth. Transfer to a fine-mesh sieve set over a large bowl; gently press the puree against the mash with the back of a wooden spoon to extract as much juice and pulp as possible, leaving the skins behind. Discard the mass in the sieve and set the puree aside. (The recipe can be made up to this point in advance—store the blueberry puree, covered, in the refrigerator for up to 2 days.)

2. Heat the milk and cream in a medium saucepan set over medium heat until tiny bubbles fizz around the pan's inner rim; adjust the heat to maintain this temperature without letting the mixture boil.

3. Beat the egg yolks and sugar in a medium bowl with a whisk or an electric mixer at medium speed until pale yellow, thick, and grainy, about 2 minutes. Whisk about a quarter of the hot milk mixture into this egg-yolk mixture until smooth, then whisk this combined mixture into the remaining hot milk mixture in the pan. Immediately reduce the heat to very low—if you're working on an electric stove, move the pan to a second burner just now set on low. Cook slowly, stirring constantly, until the mixture thickens to the consistency of melted ice cream and can coat the back of a wooden spoon, about 4 minutes. Strain through a clean fine-mesh sieve into a medium bowl to remove any bits of scrambled egg; stir in the blueberry puree, vanilla, and salt. Refrigerate until cold, for about 4 hours, or overnight.

4. While you prepare your ice cream machine, place the blueberry custard and your machine's dasher, if possible, in the freezer just to make sure they're very cold, for no more than 10 minutes.

5. Freeze the custard in your ice cream machine according to the manufacturer's instructions. Serve at once—or scoop into a large container or several small ones, seal tightly, and store in the freezer for up to 1 month; soften at room temperature for up to 10 minutes before serving.

Customize it!

Mix ⅔ cup of any of the following, or any combination of the following, into the machine just before the gelato sets, or stir into the finished gelato as it's placed in a storage container: Cap'n Crunch cereal, chopped dried apricots, chopped dried bananas, chopped dried strawberries, chopped unsalted macadamia nuts, crumbled graham crackers, crumbled ice cream sugar cones, crushed peppermint candy, dried cherries, granola, raisins, slivered almonds, or sweetened shredded coconut.

CASSATA GELATO

Makes about 1 quart (can be doubled for half-gallon machines)

Here's a traditional Sicilian gelato, made to taste something like cassata cake or zuppa inglese, both popular in Italian bakeries in the United States. The cake and glacéed fruit are usually soaked in Strega (a mint, fennel, and saffron aperitif), but use brandy if you prefer.

> 2 cups whole milk
> ½ cup heavy cream
> 6 large egg yolks, at room temperature
> ⅔ cup sugar
> 1 teaspoon vanilla extract
> ¼ teaspoon salt
> Three 1-inch-thick slices sponge or pound cake, cut into 2-inch cubes
> ½ cup chopped glacéed fruit or chopped candied orange peel
> 2 tablespoons Strega or brandy

1. Heat the milk and cream in a medium saucepan set over medium heat until tiny bubbles frizzle along the pan's inside rim. Adjust the heat so the mixture stays this hot but doesn't boil.

2. Beat the egg yolks and sugar in a medium bowl with a whisk or an electric mixer at medium speed until gooey and pale yellow, even if a little gritty, about 2 minutes. Whisk in about half of the hot milk mixture until smooth, then whisk this combined mixture back into the pan with the remaining hot milk mixture. Instantly turn the heat down to very low—if you're working on an electric stove, it's best to move the pan to a second, unused burner just now set on low. Cook slowly, stirring all the while, until the mixture thickens to the consistency of wet pancake batter and can coat the back of a wooden spoon, about 5 minutes. Strain through a fine-mesh sieve into a clean bowl to remove any bits of scrambled egg; stir in the vanilla and salt. Refrigerate until cold, for about 4 hours, or overnight.

3. Just before you make the gelato, place the custard and your ice cream machine's dasher, if possible, in the freezer to assure they're cold, for no more than 10 minutes.

4. Freeze the custard in your ice cream machine according to the manufacturer's instructions. While the custard is freezing, place the cake and dried fruit or orange peel in a medium bowl; toss with the Strega or brandy.

5. When the gelato has set but is still a little soft, stop the machine and either stir in the cake and candied fruit by hand or transfer the gelato to a storage container and stir in the cake mixture. Serve at once. Store in the freezer, tightly covered, for up to 2 weeks; soften at room temperature for up to 10 minutes before serving.

Customize it!

Substitute any of the following liqueurs for the Strega or brandy: an almond-flavored liqueur such as Amaretto, a cherry-flavored liqueur such as Cherry Heering, cinnamon schnapps, a coffee-flavored liqueur such as Kahlúa, crème de banane, a ginger-flavored liqueur such as the Original Canton Ginger Liqueur, a hazelnut-flavored liqueur such as Frangelico, an orange-flavored liqueur such as Grand Marnier, or a raspberry-flavored liqueur such as Chambord.

You can also add this same cake, candied fruit, and alcohol mixture to other gelati, such as Almond (page 8), Cherry (page 26), Chocolate (page 30), Fig (page 46), Hazelnut (page 52), Honey (page 55), Mascarpone (page 65), or Pecan (page 77).

CHERRY GELATO

Makes about 1 quart (can be doubled for half-gallon machines)

Sweet cherries were once a rare seasonal treat—but thanks to quick-freezing methods, you can enjoy this summery gelato any time. Sweet cherries are fairly delicate, so we feel the taste balances better if we cut down the yolks and add extra cream.

> 1½ cups pitted fresh sweet cherries (about 8 ounces), or one 10-ounce
>   package frozen pitted sweet cherries, thawed
> ¼ cup light corn syrup
> 1 teaspoon lemon juice
> ⅛ teaspoon salt
> 1¾ cups whole milk
> ½ cup heavy cream
> 3 large egg yolks, at room temperature
> ½ cup sugar

1. Place the cherries, corn syrup, lemon juice, and salt in a food processor fitted with the chopping blade or a wide-canister blender. Process or blend until fairly smooth—some bits of cherry skin will still be visible. Strain through a fine-mesh sieve into a bowl, pushing the puree against the mesh with the back of a wooden spoon just so the pulp and juice get through. You should have about 1¼ cups cherry puree. Set aside. (The recipe can be made up to this point in advance; store the cherry puree, covered, in your refrigerator for up to 2 days.)

2. Heat the milk and cream in a medium saucepan set over medium heat until small bubbles appear around the pan's inner rim; do not boil.

3. Meanwhile, beat the egg yolks and sugar in a medium bowl with a whisk or an electric mixer at medium speed until thick and light yellow, about 2 minutes. Whisk in about a third of the hot milk mixture until smooth, then whisk this combined mixture into the remaining hot milk mixture in the pan. Immediately reduce the heat to very low—if you're working on an electric stove, transfer the

pan to a second burner just now set on low. Cook slowly, stirring constantly, until the mixture thickens enough to coat the back of a wooden spoon, to the consistency of melted ice cream, about 5 minutes. Strain through a clean fine-mesh sieve into a second bowl; stir in the prepared cherry puree until smooth. Refrigerate until well chilled, for at least 4 hours, or overnight.

4. Before you make the cherry gelato, place the custard and your ice cream machine's dasher, if possible, in the freezer just to make sure they're very cold, for no more than 10 minutes.

5. Freeze the custard in your ice cream machine according to the manufacturer's instructions. Serve at once—or scoop into a large container or several smaller ones, seal well, and store in the freezer for up to 1 month; soften at room temperature for up to 10 minutes before serving.

Black Forest Gelato   Stir ⅓ cup crumbled chocolate fudge cookies, ⅓ cup dried cherries, and ⅓ cup mini marshmallows into the almost set gelato in the machine or into the set gelato as it's placed in a storage container.

Cherry Almond Gelato   Add ½ teaspoon almond extract with the vanilla; add ½ cup chopped toasted almonds to the chilled custard just before it's frozen.

Cherry Malt Gelato   Before adding the heated milk and cream mixture to the egg yolks, stir in ¼ cup malt powder, just until dissolved.

Cherry Pie Gelato   Add 1 teaspoon ground cinnamon and ¼ teaspoon almond extract with the vanilla; add ⅔ cup crumbled ginger snap cookies to the machine just before the gelato firms up or to the finished gelato as it's put in a storage container.

Cherry Vanilla Cookie Gelato   Add 1 cup crushed vanilla-cream sandwich cookies to the machine just before the gelato sets or to the finished gelato in a storage container.

Cherry White Chocolate Crunch Gelato   Add ½ cup white chocolate chips and ⅓ cup chopped walnut pieces to the almost firm gelato in the machine or add them to the finished gelato as it's placed in a storage container.

CHESTNUT GELATO

Makes about 1 quart (can be doubled for half-gallon machines)

Although this rich gelato may start a winter holiday tradition in your home, don't wait until you can roast chestnuts on the open fire to make this treat. Use candied chestnuts in heavy syrup, an Italian variation of a French classic called *marrons glacées*. They're available at many gourmet stores and most Italian markets.

> **One 14.8-ounce (420-gram) jar candied chestnuts in syrup**
> **⅓ cup sugar**
> **⅛ teaspoon salt**
> **6 large egg yolks, at room temperature**
> **2½ cups whole milk**
> **¼ cup heavy cream**

1. Place the chestnuts and all their syrup, the sugar, and salt in a food processor fitted with the chopping blade or a wide-canister blender; process or blend until smooth, scraping down the sides as necessary. Add the yolks and process or blend until smooth, about 1 minute. Set aside.

2. Heat the milk and cream in a medium saucepan set over medium heat until small bubbles line the pan's inside rim. Do not boil.

3. With the food processor or blender running, dribble half of this hot milk mixture through the feed tube or the center hole in the lid, processing or blending it until smooth. Whisk this combined mixture into the saucepan with the remaining milk mixture and place it over very low heat. Cook slowly, stirring all the while, until the mixture looks like smooth cake batter and can coat the back of a wooden spoon, about 5 minutes. Strain through a fine-mesh sieve into a bowl, pressing gently with a wooden spoon to make sure you get chestnut pulp into the bowl without getting any scrambled eggs in there. Refrigerate until cold, for about 4 hours, or overnight.

4. As you prepare your ice cream machine, place the chestnut custard and your machine's dasher, if possible, in the freezer to make sure they're very cold, for no more than 10 minutes.

5. Freeze the custard in your ice cream machine according to the manufacturer's instructions. Serve at once—or transfer to a large container or several small ones, seal well, and store in the freezer for up to 1 month; soften at room temperature for up to 10 minutes before serving.

Customize it!
Substitute honey or maple sugar for the sugar.

After the custard has been strained and before it's refrigerated, stir in any of the following or any combination of the following: 2 tablespoons chopped crystallized ginger, 1 teaspoon ground cinnamon, ¼ teaspoon ground mace, ¼ teaspoon ground nutmeg, or ⅛ teaspoon ground allspice.

And/or add ⅔ cup of any of the following to the machine just before the gelato sets or stir ⅔ cup into the finished gelato as it's placed into a storage container: chocolate chips, chopped dried figs, chopped pecans, chopped pitted dates, chopped purchased fruitcake, crumbled gingersnap cookies, dried cherries, mini marshmallows, or pumpkin seeds.

CHOCOLATE GELATO

Makes about 1 quart (can be doubled for half-gallon machines)

Everything hinges on the quality of chocolate you use for this sophisticated gelato. Look for brands without hydrogenated oil—better quality will yield a more sophisticated taste.

> 3 ounces unsweetened chocolate, chopped
>
> 3 large egg yolks, at room temperature
>
> 1 cup sugar
>
> 2½ cups whole milk
>
> ¼ cup heavy cream
>
> 1 teaspoon vanilla extract
>
> ⅛ teaspoon salt

1. Place the chocolate in the top half of a double boiler set over about 1 inch of simmering water, or place the chocolate in a medium bowl that fits snugly over a medium saucepan with a similar amount of simmering water. Stir until half the chocolate has melted, then remove the top half of the double boiler or the bowl from the heat (be very careful of any escaping steam) and continue stirring until the chocolate has fully melted. Set aside to cool for 5 minutes. (Alternatively, you can melt the chocolate in the microwave: place it in a medium bowl, then microwave on high in 15-second increments, stirring after each, until a little over half the chocolate has melted; continue stirring outside the microwave oven until the chocolate fully melts, then cool as directed.)

2. Beat the egg yolks and sugar in a medium bowl with either a whisk or an electric mixer at medium speed until thick and batter-like, even if still gritty, about 2 minutes. Whisk or beat the melted chocolate into the egg-yolk mixture until grainy but fairly smooth. Set aside.

3. Place the milk and cream in a medium saucepan set over medium-low heat until small bubbles appear around the inner edge of the pan. Do not boil.

4. Whisking all the while, pour about a quarter of the hot milk mixture into the chocolate mixture. Whisk this combined mixture back into the pan with the remaining milk mixture until smooth. Immediately turn the heat to very low; if you have an electric stove, use a different burner just now set on low. Cook, stirring all the while, until the mixture thickens enough to coat the back of a wooden spoon, about 2 minutes. Strain the chocolate custard through a fine-mesh sieve into a medium bowl; stir in the vanilla and salt. Refrigerate for at least 4 hours, or overnight, stirring once in a while to assure the chocolate is evenly distributed in the mixture.

5. Just before making the gelato, place the custard and, if possible, your ice cream machine's dasher, in the freezer for 10 minutes to chill them both considerably.

6. Freeze the custard in your ice cream machine according to the manufacturer's instructions. Serve at once—or transfer to a separate container or containers, seal well, and store in the freezer for up to 1 month; soften at room temperature for up to 10 minutes before serving.

Chocolate Swirl Gelato   When the gelato comes out of the machine and is placed in a large storage container, layer it with 1 cup purchased chocolate sauce, caramel sauce, or marshmallow ice cream topping, spreading one of these sauces in 3 or 4 thin layers between the layers of gelato in the container.

Rocky Road Gelato   Add ½ cup mini marshmallows and ½ cup chopped almonds or chopped walnuts to the machine just before the gelato firms up, or stir them into the finished gelato as it's transferred to a storage container.

Customize it!
Add ⅔ cup of any of the following, or any combination of the following, to the ice cream machine just before the gelato firms up, or stir them into the finished gelato in a storage container: banana chips, chocolate chips, chopped Baby Ruth bars, chopped Butterfinger bars, chopped hazelnuts, chopped Junior Mints, chopped peanut brittle, chopped pecans, chopped pistachios, chopped Twix bars, chopped unsalted macadamia nuts, chopped unsalted peanuts, chopped walnuts, Cracker Jack, crumbled biscotti, crumbled

chocolate chip cookies, crumbled macaroons, crumbled peanut butter cream sandwich cookies, dried cherries, dried cranberries, M&M's Mini Baking Bits, malted milk balls, mint chocolate chips, peanut butter chips, sweetened shredded coconut, or white chocolate chips.

CINNAMON GELATO

Makes about 1 quart (can be doubled for half-gallon machines)

Cinnamon gelato is sure to perk up a fresh apricot pie or a Thanksgiving cranberry-apple crisp—or serve it as part of a duo alongside Pecan Gelato (page 77) or Bacio Gelato (page 15).

    2¼ cups whole milk
    ¼ cup heavy cream
    Four 4-inch cinnamon sticks
    5 large egg yolks, at room temperature
    ½ cup granulated sugar
    2 tablespoons packed light brown sugar
    ¼ teaspoon salt

1. Heat the milk and cream in a medium saucepan set over medium heat until small bubbles appear around the pan's inner rim. Stir in the cinnamon sticks, remove from the heat, cover, and steep for at least 15 minutes, or up to 30 minutes, depending on how strong you want the cinnamon taste.

2. Beat the egg yolks, granulated sugar, and brown sugar in a medium bowl with a whisk or an electric mixer at medium speed until thick, about 2 minutes. The sugar will not dissolve completely, but the mixture should soften until it's grainy but gooey. Set aside.

3. Remove the cinnamon sticks, either by scooping them out with a large spoon or picking them out with tongs. Bring the milk mixture back to a bare simmer over low heat.

4. Whisking all the while, beat about half of the hot milk mixture into the egg-yolk mixture until smooth. Whisk this combined mixture back into the pan with the remaining milk mixture. Immediately reduce the heat to very low; if you have an electric stove, set the pan over a second burner just now set on low. Cook and stir

constantly until the mixture thickens to the consistency of very wet pancake batter, turns a little foamy, and can coat the back of a wooden spoon, about 6 minutes. Strain through a fine-mesh sieve into a clean, dry bowl; stir in the salt. Refrigerate until well chilled, for at least 4 hours, or overnight.

5. Just before making the gelato, it's best to shock the custard even colder by placing it and your ice cream machine's dasher, if possible, in the freezer for no more than 10 minutes.

6. Freeze the custard in your ice cream machine according to the manufacturer's instructions. Serve at once—or transfer to a large container or individual serving containers, seal tightly, and store in the freezer for up to 1 month; soften at room temperature for up to 10 minutes before serving.

Cinnamon Apple Pie Gelato Mix ½ cup chopped dried apples and ½ cup crumbled sugar wafer cookies into the machine just before the gelato firms up or stir them into the finished gelato as it's put in a storage container.

Cinnamon Coffee Cake Gelato Stir ¾ cup cubed purchased coffee cake and ¼ cup chopped walnuts into the finished gelato as it's transferred to a storage container.

Cinnamon Cookie-Dough Gelato Gently stir 1 cup crumbled, purchased, ready-to-bake cookie dough into finished gelato as it's placed in a storage container.

Cinnamon Crunch Gelato Mix ⅔ cup crushed peanut brittle or almond brittle into the chilled custard before it's frozen in the machine.

Cinnamon Date Ginger Gelato Mix ½ cup chopped pitted dates and 2 tablespoons finely chopped crystallized ginger into the chilled custard before it's frozen in the machine.

Cinnamon Oatmeal Cookie Gelato Add 1 cup crumbled oatmeal cookies to the machine just before the gelato firms up or stir them into the finished gelato as it's put in a container.

Cinnamon Raisin Granola Gelato   Mix ½ cup purchased granola and ⅓ cup raisins into the machine just before the gelato firms up or into the finished gelato as it's put in a storage container.

Cinnamon Walnut Gelato   Mix ½ cup chopped walnuts into the chilled custard just before you freeze it.

Coconut Gelato

Makes about 1 quart (can be doubled for half-gallon machines)

Here's a decadent treat that's sure to be a hit at your next backyard barbecue—or luau! Don't use either light coconut milk, which can result in an icy gelato, or cream of coconut, a sweetened cocktail concoction.

> **5 large egg yolks, at room temperature**
> **½ cup sugar**
> **One 14-ounce can unsweetened coconut milk**
> **1 cup whole milk**
> **¼ teaspoon salt**

1. Beat the egg yolks and sugar in a medium bowl using a whisk or an electric mixer at medium speed until thick and satiny, even if still grainy, about 2 minutes. Set aside.

2. If the coconut solids have solidified in the can, use a whisk to reincorporate them before stirring the coconut milk into the whole milk in a medium saucepan. Set the pan over medium heat and bring the mixture to the barest simmer, just small bubbles along the pan's inner rim.

3. Beat about a third of the hot coconut mixture into the egg-yolk mixture until smooth. Then whisk this combined mixture back into the remaining coconut mixture in the pan. Instantly reduce the heat to very low—if you have an electric stove, use a second burner you've just now turned on low. Cook slowly, stirring all the while, until the mixture rises up slightly in the pan, smells a little eggy, and thickens just enough to coat the back of a wooden spoon, about 3 minutes. Strain through a fine-mesh sieve into a second bowl and stir in the salt. Refrigerate until cold, for at least 4 hours, or overnight.

4. Ten minutes before you make the coconut gelato, place the custard and your ice cream machine's dasher, if possible, in the freezer to get them really cold.

5. Freeze the custard in your ice cream machine according to the manufacturer's instructions. Serve at once—or transfer to a large container or individual-serving containers, seal tightly, and store in the freezer for up to 1 month; soften at room temperature for up to 10 minutes before serving.

Coconut Banana Gelato Add 1 tablespoon crème de banane liqueur to the strained custard before you refrigerate it; add ⅔ cup diced dried bananas to the machine just before the gelato firms up or to the finished gelato as it's put in a storage container.

Coconut Chocolate Macaroon Gelato Add ¾ cup crumbled chocolate coconut macaroons to the machine just before the gelato firms up or stir it into the finished gelato.

Coconut Cream Pie Gelato Add ½ cup mini marshmallows and ½ cup crumbled graham crackers to the machine just before the gelato firms up or stir them into the finished gelato.

Coconut Orange Gelato Reduce the milk by ¼ cup. Just before freezing, stir ¼ cup frozen orange juice concentrate, thawed, and 2 teaspoons finely grated orange zest into the chilled custard.

Piña Colada Gelato Just before freezing, stir ½ cup canned crushed pineapple, drained, and 2 tablespoons dark rum into the chilled custard before you freeze it.

You can also stir ½ cup mini chocolate chips into any of these custards before you freeze them.

Date Gelato

Makes about 1 quart (can be doubled for half-gallon machines)

The secret to this luscious gelato is date syrup: a honey-thick liquid of pressed dates and sugar. It's sold in many gourmet stores and most Middle Eastern markets, often under its Hebrew name, *silan*.

> 6 large egg yolks, at room temperature
> 2 tablespoons packed light brown sugar
> 2 tablespoons granulated sugar
> 1 cup date syrup
> 2 cups whole milk
> ½ cup heavy cream
> 1 teaspoon vanilla extract
> ¼ teaspoon salt

1. Beat the egg yolks, brown sugar, and granulated sugar until the consistency of thick quick-bread batter, using a whisk or an electric mixer at medium speed, about 2 minutes. Beat in the date syrup until the mixture thins to the consistency of smooth batter, about 1 minute. Set aside.

2. Place the milk and cream in a medium saucepan set over medium-low heat until small bubbles fizz around the inner edges of the pan. Do not boil.

3. Whisk about half of the hot milk mixture into the date and egg mixture until smooth, then whisk this combined mixture back into the pan with the remaining hot milk mixture. Immediately reduce the heat to very low—if you have an electric stove, turn a cool burner on low and move the pan to it. Continue cooking, stirring all the while, until the mixture rises up slightly in the pan and can coat the back of a wooden spoon, about 6 minutes. Strain through a fine-mesh sieve into a clean bowl; stir in the vanilla and salt. Refrigerate for at least 4 hours, or preferably overnight.

4. Just before making the gelato, place the date custard and, if possible, your ice cream machine's dasher in the freezer for 10 minutes to chill them both considerably.

5. Freeze the custard in your ice cream machine according to the manufacturer's instructions. Serve at once—or transfer to a separate container or individual-serving containers and store in the freezer, tightly sealed, for up to 1 month; soften at room temperature for up to 10 minutes before serving.

Customize it!

Add ¾ cup of any of the following, or any combination of the following to the machine just before the gelato firms up, or stir into the finished gelato as it's put in the storage container: broken-up ice cream sugar cones, chopped cashews, chopped chocolate candy bars, chopped dried apricots, chopped pecans, chopped pistachios, chopped walnuts, crumbled gingersnap cookies, crumbled graham crackers, crumbled oatmeal cookies, or crumbled vanilla cream sandwich cookies.

Layer the gelato in the storage container with 1 cup purchased chocolate ice cream sauce, spreading it in 3 or 4 fairly even strips between the layers of gelato.

DULCE DE LECHE GELATO

Makes about 1 quart (can be doubled for half-gallon machines)

This concoction of milk and caramelized sugar, popular everywhere Spanish is spoken, has become something of a favorite among ice cream mavens—but just wait until they try it as a gelato.

> 3 cups whole milk
> ½ cup heavy cream
> 1¼ cups sugar
> 6 large egg yolks, at room temperature
> 2 teaspoons vanilla extract
> ¼ teaspoon salt

1. Heat the milk and cream in a medium saucepan set over medium heat until small bubbles pop up all around the pan's inner edge. Adjust the heat so that the milk mixture doesn't boil but stays just at this bare simmer.

2. Place the sugar in a large, heavy-duty, high-sided saucepan and shake the pan to even out the crystals across the bottom. Set the pan over medium heat. Cook, stirring occasionally, until the sugar melts; then continue cooking without stirring until the melted sugar is golden or amber, about 3 minutes. The darker, the better— but there's a fine line between a sophisticated taste and out-and-out burned.

3. Slowly whisk the hot milk mixture into this caramelized sugar. Be careful—it will roil up in the pan, so add it slowly, whisking constantly. If some of the sugar seizes (that is, clumps into a sticky ball), continue cooking over medium heat until the mixture is smooth and caramel colored, whisking all the while. Remove the pan from the heat and set aside.

4. Whisk the egg yolks in a medium bowl until light and lemony, about 1 minute. Whisk about a third of the warm milk mixture into the yolks until smooth. Then whisk this combined mixture back into the pan with the remaining milk mixture.

Place the pan over very low heat and cook slowly until the mixture thickens somewhat, like loose pancake batter, and can coat the back of a wooden spoon, about 6 minutes. Strain through a fine-mesh sieve into a second bowl to remove any bits of cooked egg; stir in the vanilla and salt. Refrigerate until well chilled, for at least 4 hours, or preferably overnight.

5. Before you make the gelato, place the custard and the dasher from your ice cream maker, if possible, in the freezer for 10 minutes, just to get them really cold.

6. Freeze the custard in your ice cream machine according to the manufacturer's instructions. Serve at once—or scoop into one large or several smaller containers, seal tightly, and store in the freezer for up to 1 month. (Because of the large amount of sugar, the gelato will not freeze hard.)

Caramelized Dulce de Leche Gelato As the gelato comes out of the machine and into a large storage container, drizzle 1 cup purchased caramel ice cream sauce in several thin layers between the gelato layers.

Dulce de Leche Cheesecake Gelato Add ¼ cup no-bake cheesecake powder with the vanilla, stirring until it's dissolved. When the gelato's firm, stir ½ cup crumbled graham cracker cookies into it.

Dulce de Leche Coconut Chocolate Chip Gelato Mix ⅓ cup toasted sweetened shredded coconut and ½ cup semisweet or mini chocolate chips into the machine just as the gelato firms up or into the finished gelato as it's placed in a storage container.

Dulce de Leche Honey-Roasted Cashew Gelato Mix ⅔ cup chopped honey-roasted cashews into the machine just as the gelato firms up or into the finished gelato as it's placed in a storage container. (You can substitute any honey-roasted nut for this recipe.)

Dulce de Leche Truffle Ice Cream Stir ¾ cup chopped chocolate truffles into the machine just before the gelato firms up or into finished gelato as it's placed in a storage container.

EGG NOG GELATO

Makes about 1 quart (can be doubled for half-gallon machines)

Why wait for the holidays to savor the taste of egg nog? You can omit the rum and bourbon, of course—stir in 1 teaspoon rum extract in their stead.

> 8 large egg yolks, at room temperature
> ¾ cup sugar
> 2¼ cups whole milk
> ¼ cup heavy cream
> 2 tablespoons rum, preferably dark rum, such as Myers's Dark Rum
> 2 tablespoons bourbon
> 1 teaspoon vanilla extract
> 1 teaspoon grated nutmeg
> ¼ teaspoon salt

1. Beat the egg yolks and sugar in a medium bowl with a whisk or an electric mixer at medium speed until thick and pale yellow, even if not yet smooth, about 3 minutes. The beaten concoction should make satiny ribbons that do not instantly dissolve back into the mixture when the whisk or the beaters are lifted out of it. Set aside.

2. Heat the milk and cream in a medium saucepan over medium heat until barely bubbling around the pan's inner edge. Do not boil.

3. Whisking all the while, add about a third of the hot milk mixture to the beaten egg-yolk mixture until smooth. Whisk this combined mixture back into the remaining hot milk mixture. Instantly reduce the heat to very low—if you have an electric stove, use a second burner just now set to low. Cook slowly until thickened like very runny pudding, about 5 minutes. Strain through a fine-mesh sieve into a clean bowl; stir in the rum, bourbon, vanilla, nutmeg, and salt. Refrigerate until cold, for at least 4 hours, or preferably overnight.

4. Just before freezing the gelato, place the egg nog custard and your ice cream machine's dasher, if possible, in the freezer for 10 minutes to get them really chilled down.

5. Freeze the custard in your ice cream machine according to the manufacturer's instructions. Serve at once—or spoon into a large container or several single-serving ones and store in the freezer for up to 1 month; soften at room temperature for up to 10 minutes before serving.

Customize it!

Mix ⅔ cup of any of the following, or any combination of the following, into the machine just before the gelato sets, or into the finished gelato as it's put in a storage container: chocolate-covered espresso beans, chocolate-covered raisins, chopped dried bananas, chopped dried pitted dates, chopped hazelnuts, chopped honey-roasted almonds, chopped marzipan, chopped pecans, crumbled gingersnap cookies, dried cherries, golden raisins, milk chocolate chips, semisweet chocolate chips, or white chocolate chips.

ESPRESSO GELATO

Makes about 1 quart (can be doubled for half-gallon machines)

The trick here is instant espresso powder, available at many supermarkets and from outlets listed in the Source Guide (page 241). While instant coffee will work, it will not give the frozen dessert its characteristic dark, deep taste.

> 5 large egg yolks, at room temperature
> ⅔ cup granulated sugar
> 2 tablespoons packed dark brown sugar
> 2½ cups whole milk
> ⅓ cup heavy cream
> 2 tablespoons instant espresso powder
> 1 teaspoon vanilla extract
> ¼ teaspoon salt

1. Beat the egg yolks, granulated sugar, and brown sugar in a medium bowl with a whisk or an electric mixer at medium speed until the still grainy, pale brown mixture nevertheless has the texture of beaten batter, about 3 minutes. Set aside.

2. Heat the milk and cream in a medium saucepan over medium heat just until bubbles frizzle all around the pan's inner edge. Whisk in the espresso powder.

3. Whisk about a third of the hot milk mixture into the beaten egg-yolk mixture until smooth, then whisk this combined mixture into the remainder of the milk mixture in the pan. Instantly reduce the heat to very low; if you have an electric stove, use a second burner just now turned on low. Stir constantly, gently heating the custard until a few puffs of steam rise from its surface and it's thick enough to coat the back of a wooden spoon, about 5 minutes. Strain through a fine-mesh sieve into a clean bowl to remove any bits of egg that have inadvertently scrambled, taking care not to scrape out any solids that may have cooked onto the bottom of the pan. Stir in the vanilla and salt. Chill in the refrigerator for at least 4 hours, or overnight.

4. Just before you make the espresso gelato, place the custard and your ice cream machine's dasher, if possible, in the freezer for 10 minutes, just to shock them cold.

5. Freeze in your ice cream machine according to the instruction booklet. Serve at once—or transfer to a large container or individual-serving containers and store in the freezer for up to 1 month; soften at room temperature for up to 10 minutes before serving.

Espresso Biscotti Gelato   Add 1 cup crumbled biscotti to the gelato just before it firms up in the machine, or stir it into the finished gelato as it's put in the storage container.

Espresso Chocolate Raisin Gelato   Add ½ cup semisweet or mini chocolate chips and ½ cup raisins to the machine just before the gelato's finished, or stir into the finished gelato as it's put in a large storage container.

Espresso Chocolate Toffee Gelato   Add ½ cup chopped toffee candy bars, such as Heath or Skor bars, and ½ cup mini chocolate chips to the almost firm gelato in the machine or stir into the finished gelato as it's put in the storage container.

Espresso Crunch Gelato   Add ⅔ cup chocolate-covered espresso beans to the machine just before the gelato firms up, or stir into the finished gelato as it's put in the storage container.

Espresso Fudge Swirl Gelato   As the finished gelato is scooped or dispensed into a large storage container, layer it with 1 cup purchased chocolate ice cream sauce or softened but cooked hot fudge sauce.

Espresso Maple Walnut Gelato   Substitute maple sugar for the granulated sugar; stir ½ cup chopped walnuts into the machine just as the gelato firms up, or stir into the finished gelato as it comes out of the machine.

FIG GELATO

Makes about 1 quart (can be doubled for half-gallon machines)

Because the best taste comes from steeping the figs in the milk, the best fruit for this tantalizing concoction is the dried golden Calimyrna fig from California. Look for plump dried figs with no brown spots.

>   12 dried Calimyrna figs (about 6 ounces), stems removed
>   2¾ cups whole milk
>   ¼ cup heavy cream
>   6 large egg yolks, at room temperature
>   ½ cup sugar
>   ½ teaspoon vanilla extract
>   ¼ teaspoon salt

1. Place the dried figs and the milk in a large saucepan and set it over medium-high heat. Bring the mixture to a simmer, reduce the heat, and simmer very slowly for 5 minutes. Cover the pan, remove it from the heat, and steep for 30 minutes.

2. Place the milk and figs in a food processor fitted with the chopping blade or a wide-canister blender. Process or blend until smooth, scraping down the sides of the bowl as necessary. (For a note on how to deal with hot things in a blender, see page 16.) Pour this mixture into a medium saucepan; stir in the cream. Set over medium heat and bring it to the barest simmer, just little bubbles around the pan's inner rim.

3. Beat the egg yolks and sugar in a medium bowl with a whisk or an electric mixer at medium speed until pale yellow, almost beige, and thick, even if gritty, about 2 minutes. Whisk about a quarter of the hot milk mixture into the egg-yolk mixture until smooth, then whisk this combined mixture back into the remaining hot milk mixture in the pan. Immediately reduce the heat to very low—if you're working on an electric stove, move the pan to a second burner just now set on low. Cook slowly, stirring all the while, until the mixture thickens slightly, just

enough to coat the back of a wooden spoon, about 2 minutes. Strain through a fine-mesh sieve into a clean bowl; stir in the vanilla and salt. Refrigerate until cold, for about 4 hours, or overnight.

4. As you prepare your ice cream machine, place the fig custard and the machine's dasher, if possible, in the freezer to get them really cold, but for no more than 10 minutes.

5. Freeze the custard in your ice cream machine according to the manufacturer's instructions. Serve at once—or transfer to a large container or individual-serving containers, seal well, and store in the freezer for up to 1 month; soften at room temperature for up to 10 minutes before serving.

Fig, Almond, and Chocolate Gelato   Stir ½ cup toasted sliced almonds and ½ cup milk chocolate chips into the machine just before the gelato's ready, or into the finished gelato as you transfer it to a storage container.

Fig and Honey Gelato   Substitute honey for the sugar.

Fig and Maple Gelato   Substitute maple sugar for the sugar.

Fig Cookie Gelato   Substitute ½ cup crumbled cookies, such as sugar cookies, fig cookies, or shortbread, in the machine just before the gelato's ready, or stir them into the finished gelato as you put it in a large storage container.

Fig Ginger Gelato   Stir ⅓ cup finely chopped crystallized ginger to the chilled custard before freezing in the machine.

Fig Walnut Gelato   Add ¾ cup chopped walnuts to the machine just before the gelato's ready, or stir into the finished gelato as it's transferred to a storage container.

Spiced Fig Gelato   Stir in ½ teaspoon ground cinnamon, ¼ teaspoon grated nutmeg, and ⅛ teaspoon ground mace with the vanilla. Stir ¼ cup chopped candied orange rind into the chilled custard before freezing it in the machine.

FIOR DI CREMA

Makes about 1 quart (can be doubled for half-gallon machines)

Italian *gelaterie* have one flavor that bears a striking resemblance to American ice cream: *fior di crema*. It's the simplest gelato of all, made with cream as the main ingredient, not milk. If you're strictly a purist, omit the vanilla extract. This gelato is so classic, we feel variations only muddle its simplicity.

> **3 large egg yolks, at room temperature**
> **⅔ cup sugar**
> **2¼ cups heavy cream**
> **¾ cup whole milk**
> **1 teaspoon vanilla extract, optional**
> **⅛ teaspoon salt**

1. Beat the egg yolks and ⅓ cup of the sugar in a medium bowl with a whisk or an electric mixer at medium speed until gooey-grainy and lightly colored, about 2 minutes. Set aside.

2. Heat the cream and milk in a medium saucepan over medium heat until small bubbles pop up right around the pan's inner rim. Stir the remaining ⅓ cup sugar into the hot milk mixture until the sugar dissolves completely. Remove the pan from the heat.

3. Whisk about a third of the hot milk mixture into the egg-yolk mixture until smooth, then whisk the combined mixture back into the pan with the remaining warm cream mixture that's now off the heat. Whisk until smooth, then place the pan over low heat and cook slowly, stirring constantly, just until the mixture thickens slightly, about 4 minutes, maybe less. Do not bring to a simmer—simply cook until you see a change in the viscosity. Strain through a fine-mesh sieve into a clean bowl; stir in the vanilla, if using, and salt. Refrigerate until cold, for about 4 hours, or overnight.

4. While you prepare your ice cream machine, place the custard and your machine's dasher, if possible, in the freezer to make sure they're very cold, for no more than 10 minutes.

5. Freeze the custard in your ice cream machine according to the manufacturer's instructions. Serve at once—or scoop into a large, sealable container or several smaller ones that seal tightly and store in the freezer for up to 1 month; soften at room temperature for up to 10 minutes before serving.

Ginger Gelato

Makes about 1 quart (can be doubled for half-gallon machines)

The secret to smooth ginger gelato, without all those stringy ginger bits, is bottled ginger juice, available in the baking, condiment, or spice aisle of most supermarkets. You can also make your own by squeezing peeled fresh ginger through a garlic press. There's a bit more cream here to balance the spicy taste of ginger.

> **8 large egg yolks, at room temperature**
> **½ cup plus 1 tablespoon sugar**
> **2½ cups whole milk**
> **¾ cup heavy cream**
> **1½ tablespoons ginger juice**
> **¼ teaspoon salt**

1. Beat the egg yolks and sugar in a medium bowl with a whisk or an electric mixer at medium speed until pale yellow and very thick, about 2 minutes. Set aside.

2. Heat the milk and cream in a medium saucepan set over medium heat until little bubbles pop up along the pan's inner rim; adjust the heat so the mixture remains hot but does not boil.

3. Whisk about a quarter of the hot milk mixture into the egg-yolk mixture until smooth, then whisk this combined mixture back into the remaining milk mixture in the pan. Immediately reduce the heat to very low—if you're working on an electric stove, move the pan to an unused burner just now set on low. Cook slowly, stirring constantly, until the mixture is like wet but smooth cake batter and can coat the back of a wooden spoon, about 7 minutes. Strain through a fine-mesh sieve into a clean bowl to remove any bits of scrambled egg; stir in the ginger juice and salt. Refrigerate until well chilled, for about 4 hours, or overnight.

4. Just before freezing, place the custard and your ice cream machine's dasher, if possible, in the freezer for 10 minutes, just to get them cold.

5. Freeze in your ice cream machine according to the manufacturer's instructions. Serve at once—or transfer to a large container or individual-serving containers and store in the freezer, tightly sealed, for up to 1 month; soften at room temperature for up to 10 minutes before serving.

Gingerbread Gelato   Reduce the sugar to ¼ cup; add ¼ cup plus 2 tablespoons packed dark brown sugar with the remaining sugar. Stir ½ teaspoon ground cinnamon and ¼ teaspoon grated nutmeg into the strained custard before it chills. Stir ½ cup golden raisins into the chilled custard before freezing it in the machine.

Ginger Cookie Gelato   Add ⅔ cup chopped gingerbread cookies to the machine just before the gelato's ready, or stir them into the finished gelato as it's transferred to a storage container.

Ginger Cranberry Crunch Gelato   Add ½ cup dried cranberries and ½ cup crumbled oatmeal cookies to the machine just before the gelato's ready, or stir them into the finished gelato as it's transferred to a storage container.

Hazelnut Gelato

Makes about 1 quart (can be doubled for half-gallon machines)

To make this classic gelato (*nocciola* in Italian), you must first make hazelnut milk from toasted hazelnuts. If you can find hazelnut milk in a gourmet store or health-food store, omit these steps and proceed straight to making the custard, mixing 2¼ cups hazelnut milk with the cream.

> 1½ cups hazelnuts
> 3 cups whole milk, or more as necessary
> 6 large egg yolks, at room temperature
> ⅔ cup sugar
> ½ cup heavy cream
> ½ teaspoon vanilla extract
> ⅛ teaspoon salt

1. Position a rack in the center of the oven and preheat the oven to 350°F. Place the hazelnuts on a large baking sheet and toast in the oven, stirring often, until lightly browned but very aromatic, about 7 minutes. Cool on the baking sheet for 5 minutes.

2. Place the toasted hazelnuts and the milk in a medium saucepan set over medium heat. Bring the mixture to a low simmer, adjust the heat so it doesn't come to a boil, and simmer at the barest bubble for 5 minutes. Cover the pan, remove it from the heat, and set aside to steep for 20 minutes. Meanwhile, line a sieve or colander with cheesecloth and set it over a large bowl.

3. Pour the hazelnuts and milk in a food processor fitted with the chopping blade or a wide-canister blender. Process or blend until fairly smooth. (You may work in batches, if necessary. For a note about dealing with hot things in a blender, see page 16.) Pour the pureed mixture into the prepared sieve; drain for 15 minutes.

4. Gather the cheesecloth into a ball with the hazelnuts inside it. Holding it over the sieve and bowl, gently squeeze as much milk from the nuts as possible. You should

end up with about 2¼ cups hazelnut milk; if you have less, add whole milk to bring the mixture up to the desired amount.

5. Beat the egg yolks and the sugar in a medium bowl with a whisk or an electric mixer at medium speed until thick and pale yellow, about 2 minutes. Set aside.

6. Combine the hazelnut milk with the cream in a medium saucepan set over medium heat. Heat just until tiny bubbles appear around the pan's inside rim.

7. Whisk about a quarter of the hot hazelnut milk mixture into this egg-yolk mixture until smooth, then whisk this combined mixture into the remaining hot hazelnut milk mixture. Immediately reduce the heat to very low—if you're working on an electric stove, use a second burner on low, one that hasn't been previously heated. Cook slowly, stirring constantly, until the mixture thickens slightly, about like thin, wet batter, and can coat the back of a wooden spoon, about 3 minutes. Strain through a clean fine-mesh sieve into a clean bowl to remove any extraneous bits of cooked egg; stir in the vanilla and salt. Refrigerate until cold, for about 4 hours, or overnight.

8. While you prepare your ice cream machine, place the hazelnut custard and the machine's dasher, if possible, in the freezer to assure that they're very cold, for no more than 10 minutes.

9. Freeze in your ice cream machine according to the manufacturer's instructions. Serve at once—or transfer to a large container or individual-serving-size containers, seal tightly, and store in the freezer for up to 1 month; soften at room temperature for up to 10 minutes before serving.

Hazelnut Coffee Gelato   Reduce the milk to 2¾ cups. Stir ¼ cup coffee-flavored liqueur, such as Kahlúa, into the strained custard with the vanilla.

Hazelnut Fudge Gelato   As the finished gelato is transferred to a storage container, make 3 or 4 layers with 1 cup purchased, softened, and cooled hot fudge sauce or 1 cup purchased chocolate sauce in between layers of gelato, thereby making ribbons of chocolate in the gelato.

Hazelnut Orange Gelato   Reduce the milk to 2¾ cups. Stir ¼ cup orange-flavored liqueur, such as Grand Marnier, into the strained custard with the vanilla.

Hazelnut Raspberry Swirl Gelato   Soften 1 cup purchased raspberry jam by placing it in a small saucepan over low heat and stirring until spreadable, about 1 minute. Set aside to cool for 5 minutes. Once the gelato's ready, layer this jam in 3 or 4 strips through the gelato as it's spooned or dispensed into a storage container.

Customize it!
Mix ⅔ cup of any of the following, or any combination of the following, into the machine just before the gelato's ready, or stir into the finished gelato as it's transferred to a container: butterscotch chips, chopped dried bananas, chopped dried figs, chopped pitted dates, crumbled gingersnap cookies, crumbled graham crackers, crumbled shortbread, dried cherries, dried cranberries, semisweet chocolate chips, or white chocolate chips.

HONEY GELATO

Makes about 1 quart (can be doubled for half-gallon machines)

The darker the honey, the more intense the taste of this creamy gelato—so choose a variety like wildflower, chestnut, oak, star thistle, or even pine tree, available at most gourmet markets and from outlets listed in the Source Guide (page 241).

> **6 large egg yolks, at room temperature**
> **⅓ cup honey, preferably a dark honey**
> **2 tablespoons sugar**
> **2½ cups whole milk**
> **3 tablespoons heavy cream**
> **¼ teaspoon salt**

1. Beat the egg yolks, honey, and sugar with a whisk or an electric mixer at medium speed until quite thick and pale yellow, but not until the mixture makes ribbons when dripped off the whisk or beaters, about 3 minutes. Set aside.

2. Heat the milk and cream in a medium saucepan over medium heat until small bubbles fizz around the pan's inner rim; do not boil but adjust the heat to maintain these bubbles.

3. Beat about a quarter of the hot milk mixture into the egg-yolk mixture until smooth, then beat this combined mixture back into the remaining hot milk mixture in the pan. Immediately reduce the heat to very low—move the pan to an unused burner just now set on low if you're working with an electric stove. Cook slowly, stirring all the while, until the mixture thickens somewhat, turns foamy, and can coat the back of a wooden spoon, about 6 minutes. Strain through a fine-mesh sieve into a clean bowl; stir in the salt. Refrigerate until well chilled, for about 4 hours, or overnight.

4. While you prepare your ice cream machine, place the custard and your machine's dasher, if possible, in the freezer, just to shock them cold, for no more than 10 minutes.

5. Freeze the custard in your ice cream machine according to the manufacturer's instructions. Serve at once—or store in a single sealable container or several individual-serving containers in the freezer for up to 1 month; soften at room temperature for up to 10 minutes before serving.

Customize it!
Add any of the following with the salt: 2 teaspoons vanilla extract, 2 teaspoons orange extract, 1 teaspoon lemon extract, or 1 teaspoon rum extract.

And/or add ¾ cup of any of the following, or any combination of the following, to the machine just before the gelato's ready, or stir into the finished gelato as it's scooped or dispensed into a storage container: chopped cashews, chopped dried apples, chopped dried apricots, chopped dried dates, chopped dried figs, chopped dried pears, chopped hazelnuts, chopped pecans, chopped pistachios, chopped unsalted peanuts, chopped walnuts, cocoa nibs, dried cherries, dried cranberries, or raisins.

LEMON GELATO

Makes about 1 quart (can be doubled for half-gallon machines)

Lemon extract is available in the baking aisle of some supermarkets, at most specialty baking stores, and from outlets listed in the Source Guide (page 241). Do not use lemon oil; it will overpower the custard. The milder extract gives this creamy gelato the tart taste of a lemon meringue pie.

> **8 large egg yolks, at room temperature**
> **¾ cup sugar**
> **2½ cups whole milk**
> **¼ cup heavy cream**
> **¼ cup lemon juice**
> **1 tablespoon lemon extract**
> **½ teaspoon vanilla extract**
> **¼ teaspoon salt**

1. Beat the egg yolks and sugar in a medium bowl with a whisk or an electric mixer at medium speed until thick and satiny, even if still grainy, about 2 minutes. Set aside.

2. Heat the milk and cream in a medium saucepan set over medium heat until small bubbles simmer around the pan's inner rim; do not boil.

3. Whisk about half of the hot milk mixture into the egg-yolk mixture until smooth, then whisk this mixture into the remaining hot milk mixture in the pan. Immediately reduce the heat to very low—or set the pan over a second burner just now set on low if you're working on an electric stove. Cook slowly, stirring constantly, until the mixture thickens slightly, just so it coats the back of a wooden spoon, about 5 minutes. Stir in the lemon juice. Strain through a fine-mesh sieve into a clean bowl to remove any bits of scrambled egg; stir in the lemon extract, vanilla, and salt. Refrigerate until cold, for about 4 hours, or overnight.

4. As you prepare your ice cream machine, place the lemon custard and your machine's dasher, if possible, in the freezer to assure they're both very cold, but no more than 10 minutes.

5. Freeze the custard in your ice cream machine according to the manufacturer's instructions. Serve at once—or transfer to a large container or several smaller ones, seal well, and store in the freezer for up to 1 month; soften at room temperature for up to 10 minutes before serving.

Lemon Cheesecake Gelato   Stir ¼ cup instant no-bake cheesecake powder into the chilled custard before freezing it in the machine.

Lemon Mint Gelato   Replace the vanilla with ¼ teaspoon mint or peppermint extract.

Lemon Poppy Seed Gelato   Stir 2 tablespoons poppy seeds into the custard with the vanilla.

Lemon Strawberry Swirl Gelato   As the gelato is spooned or dispensed into a storage container, drizzle 1 cup purchased strawberry ice cream topping into the gelato in three or four additions, thereby making thin layers of the sauce.

Customize it!
Mix ⅔ cup of any of the following, or any combination of the following, into the machine just before the gelato firms up, or stir into the finished gelato as it's placed into a storage container: chopped dried mango, chopped dried pineapple, crumbled gingersnap cookies, granola, mini marshmallows, raisins, or unsalted sunflower seeds.

LIME GELATO

Makes about 1 quart (can be doubled for half-gallon machines)

Think of this as a frozen version of an old-fashioned, cream-topped, icebox pie: tart and ever so refreshing.

> **8 large egg yolks, at room temperature**
> **¾ cup plus 2 tablespoons sugar**
> **Grated zest of 1 lime**
> **1¾ cups whole milk**
> **¼ cup heavy cream**
> **¾ cup plus 2 tablespoons lime juice**
> **¼ teaspoon salt**

1. Beat the egg yolks, sugar, and lime zest in a medium bowl with a whisk or an electric mixer at medium speed until thick and pale, even if still grainy, about 2 minutes. Set aside.

2. Heat the milk and cream in a medium saucepan set over medium heat until small bubbles appear along the pan's inner rim; do not boil.

3. Whisk about a quarter of the hot milk mixture into the egg-yolk mixture until smooth, then whisk this combined mixture into the remaining hot milk mixture still in the pan. Immediately reduce the heat to very low—or move the pan to a second burner now set on low if you're working on an electric stove. Cook slowly, stirring all the while, until the mixture thickens to the consistency of smooth, wet cake batter and can coat the back of a wooden spoon, about 6 minutes. Whisk in the lime juice, then strain the mixture through a fine-mesh sieve into a clean bowl to remove any extraneous bits of cooked egg, lime zest, or pulp. Stir in the salt. Refrigerate until cold, for about 4 hours, or overnight.

4. Just before you make the lime gelato, place the custard and your ice cream machine's dasher, if possible, in the freezer to assure they're very cold, for no more than 10 minutes.

5. Freeze the custard in your ice cream machine according to the manufacturer's instructions. Serve at once—or scoop into a large container or several smaller ones, seal tightly, and store in the freezer for up to 1 month; soften at room temperature for up to 10 minutes before serving.

Lime Coconut Rum Gelato   Reduce the milk to ¾ cup; add 1 cup coconut milk with the remaining milk. Stir in 1 teaspoon rum extract with the salt.

Daiquiri Gelato   Reduce the milk to 1½ cups. Add ⅓ cup white rum with the salt.

Tangerine Gelato   Substitute the zest of a medium tangerine and tangerine juice for the lime zest and juice.

MANGO GELATO

Makes about 1 quart (can be doubled for half-gallon machines)

Mangos are so perfumy, they're a natural in gelato. Choose brightly colored, mottled mangos that smell irresistible.

> 2 large ripe mangos, peeled, pitted, and chopped
> 2 teaspoons lime juice
> ¼ teaspoon salt
> 4 large egg yolks, at room temperature
> 1 cup sugar
> 1¾ cups whole milk
> ¼ cup heavy cream

1. Place the chopped mango, lime juice, and salt in a food processor fitted with the chopping blade or a wide-canister blender; process or blend until smooth. Pour this mixture into a fine-mesh strainer and gently push it through the mesh and into a medium bowl with the back of a wooden spoon, thereby removing the stringy bits from the mango pulp. You should end up with about 1¼ cups smooth mango puree. Set aside.

2. Beat the egg yolks and sugar in a medium bowl with a whisk or an electric mixer at medium speed until thick and pale, if still grainy, about 2 minutes. Set aside.

3. Heat the milk and cream in a medium saucepan just until small bubbles appear at the pan's inner rim; adjust the heat so the mixture does not boil.

4. Whisk about half of the hot milk mixture into the beaten egg yolks until smooth, then whisk this combined mixture back into the pan with the remaining hot milk mixture. Immediately reduce the heat to very low—if you're working with an electric stove, transfer the pan to an unused burner just now set on low. Cook slowly, stirring all the while, until the mixture is the consistency of melted ice cream and can coat the back of a wooden spoon, about 7 minutes. Strain through

a fine-mesh sieve into a clean bowl; stir in the prepared mango puree. Refrigerate until cold, for about 4 hours, or overnight.

5. As you prepare your ice cream machine, place the mango custard and the machine's dasher, if possible, in the freezer, just to assure they're really cold, for no more than 10 minutes.

6. Freeze the custard in your ice cream machine according to the manufacturer's instructions. Serve at once—or transfer to a large container or several smaller ones, seal tightly, and store in the freezer for up to 1 month; soften at room temperature for up to 10 minutes before serving.

Mango Banana Gelato   Use only 1 mango. Add 1 large ripe peeled banana to the food processor with the remaining mango. Add 1 teaspoon vanilla with the lime juice.

Mango Ginger Gelato   Stir 1 tablespoon ginger juice into the strained custard before it's refrigerated.

Mango Rum Gelato   Reduce the milk to 1½ cups. Add 1 additional large egg yolk. Stir ¼ cup dark rum into the mango puree. If desired, stir ½ cup sweetened shredded coconut, toasted, into the gelato just as it firms up in the machine.

Maple Gelato

Makes about 1 quart (can be doubled for half-gallon machines)

Maple syrup is sold in two grades: A and B. The latter is used in commercial baking and proves too strong for gelato. Grade A comes in three varieties—light amber, medium amber, and dark amber. For the best maple gelato, use Grade A medium amber or dark amber, not the more delicate light amber.

1 cup maple syrup, preferably Grade A medium or dark amber
5 large egg yolks, at room temperature
2¼ cups whole milk
¼ cup heavy cream
¼ teaspoon salt

1. Beat the maple syrup and egg yolks with a whisk or an electric mixer until thick and pale, about 2 minutes. Set aside.

2. Heat the milk and cream in a medium saucepan over medium heat until tiny bubbles pop up around the pan's inner edge. Do not boil.

3. Whisk about a third of the hot milk mixture into the egg-yolk mixture until smooth, then whisk this combined mixture into the remaining hot milk mixture in the pan. Immediately reduce the heat to very low—if you're working on an electric stove, move the pan to an unused burner just now set on low. Cook slowly, stirring constantly, until the mixture begins to get foamy, starts to smell eggy, and can coat the back of a wooden spoon, about 6 minutes. Strain through a fine-mesh sieve into a second bowl to remove any little bits of scrambled egg; stir in the salt. Refrigerate until well chilled, for about 4 hours, or overnight.

4. Just before you make the maple gelato, place the custard and your ice cream machine's dasher, if possible, in the freezer to assure they are very cold, for no more than 10 minutes.

5. Freeze the custard in your ice cream machine according to the manufacturer's instructions. Serve at once—or transfer to a large container or several individual-serving containers, seal tightly, and store in the freezer for up to 1 month; soften at room temperature for up to 10 minutes before serving.

Customize it!

Add ½ cup of any of the following to the machine when the gelato is almost ready, or stir into the finished gelato as you spoon it into a large storage container: chopped toasted hazelnuts, chopped toasted pecans, chopped toasted pine nuts, chopped unsalted cashews, chopped toasted walnuts, sliced almonds, or toasted unsalted pumpkin seeds.

Or mix ⅔ cup of any of the following, or any combination of the following, using the same method as above: chocolate chip cookies, chocolate-covered espresso beans, cocoa nibs, crumbled gingersnap cookies, crumbled graham crackers, crumbled sugar wafer cookies, crumbled waffle ice cream cones, dried cranberries, granola, Grape-Nuts cereal, M&M's Mini Baking Bits, raisins, ready-to-bake chocolate chip cookie dough, semisweet chocolate chips, or white chocolate chips.

MASCARPONE GELATO

Makes about 1 quart (can be doubled for half-gallon machines)

Here's a decadent treat made with a soft cheese originally from Lombardy, a gorgeous northern Italian region famed for its lakes and mountains. For the best taste, let the cheese sit out at room temperature for 1 hour before making the custard.

> 4 large egg yolks, at room temperature
>
> ½ cup sugar
>
> 2 cups whole milk
>
> 8 ounces mascarpone cheese (about 1 cup), at room temperature
>
> ½ teaspoon vanilla extract

1. Beat the egg yolks and sugar in a medium bowl with a whisk or an electric mixer at medium speed until quite thick and grainy but lightly colored, about 2 minutes. Set aside.

2. Heat the milk in a medium saucepan set over medium heat until small bubbles dot the pan's inner edges. Adjust the heat so the milk does not boil.

3. Whisk about half of the hot milk into the egg-yolk mixture until smooth, then whisk this combined mixture back into the pan with the remaining hot milk. Immediately reduce the heat to very low; if you're using an electric stove, place the pan on a second burner that has just been turned to low. Cook slowly, stirring all the while, until the mixture gets a little foamy and can coat the back of a wooden spoon, about 5 minutes. Strain through a fine-mesh sieve into a clean bowl to get rid of any bits of scrambled egg; whisk in the cheese and vanilla until smooth. Place in the refrigerator and chill thoroughly, for about 4 hours, or overnight.

4. Ten minutes before you're ready to make the gelato, place the custard and your ice cream's dasher, if possible, in the freezer, just to shock them very cold.

5. Freeze the custard in your ice cream machine according to the manufacturer's instructions. Serve at once—or transfer to a large container or several individual-

serving containers and store in the freezer, tightly sealed, for up to 1 month; soften at room temperature for up to 10 minutes before serving.

Customize it!

Add 1½ teaspoons lemon extract, 1½ teaspoons orange extract, 1 teaspoon anise extract, 1 teaspoon maple extract, or 1 teaspoon rum extract with the vanilla.

And/or add ⅔ cup finely diced apricots, finely diced dried figs, finely diced pitted dates (preferably a soft date such as Medjool), or raisins to the chilled custard just before freezing it in the machine.

MINT GELATO

Makes about 1 quart (can be doubled for half-gallon machines)

Making mint gelato is an exercise in balance. Adding the extract just before freezing prevents the custard from being overpowered—and keeps everything in your refrigerator from smelling like mint.

> **7 large egg yolks, at room temperature**
> **⅔ cup sugar**
> **2½ cups whole milk**
> **⅔ cup heavy cream**
> **¼ teaspoon salt**
> **½ teaspoon mint extract, or more to taste, but no more than 1 teaspoon**
> **2 drops green food coloring, optional**

1. Beat the egg yolks and sugar in a medium bowl, using a whisk or an electric mixer at medium speed, until thick, even if still grainy, but lemony in color, about 2 minutes. Set aside.

2. Heat the milk and cream in a medium saucepan set over medium heat until small bubbles appear around the edges of the pan; adjust the heat so the milk doesn't boil.

3. Whisk about a third of the heated milk and cream into the egg-yolk mixture until smooth, then whisk this combined mixture back into the pan with the remaining milk and cream. Reduce the heat to low at once; if you're using an electric stove, use a second burner that's just now been turned to low. Cook slowly, stirring all the while, until the mixture thickens somewhat, about like smooth, very wet cake batter, and can coat the back of a wooden spoon, about 5 minutes. Strain into a clean bowl through a fine-mesh sieve to remove any extraneous bits of cooked egg; stir in the salt. Refrigerate until cold, for about 4 hours, or overnight.

4. Just before you're ready to make the gelato, place the custard and your ice cream machine's dasher, if possible, in the freezer for no more than 10 minutes.

5. Stir the mint extract and the green food coloring, if using, into the custard. Freeze in your ice cream machine according to the manufacturer's instructions. Serve at once—or transfer to a large container or small, single-serving containers and store in the freezer, tightly covered, for up to 1 month; soften at room temperature for up to 10 minutes before serving.

Grasshopper Gelato   Reduce the milk to 2¼ cups. Add 1 additional large egg yolk. Stir in ¼ cup white crème de cacao with the mint extract.

Mint Chocolate Chip Gelato   Add ¾ cup mini chocolate chips, white chocolate chips, or shaved semisweet chocolate to the machine when the gelato's almost finished, or to the finished gelato when you pack it into a large container for storage.

Mint Fudge Swirl Gelato   As you transfer the gelato to a large container, drizzle 1 cup purchased, softened, and cooled hot fudge sauce or purchased chocolate sauce in three or four thin layers over the gelato layers, making thin ribbons of chocolate in the gelato.

Mint Nibs Gelato   Mix ⅔ cup cocoa nibs into the chilled custard before freezing.

MOCHA GELATO

Makes about 1 quart (can be doubled for half-gallon machines)

Originally, mocha referred to a particular kind of coffee bean produced on the Arabian peninsula and shipped through Mocha, Yemen. It became something of a European fad at about the same time chocolate became its own *cause célèbre*. Together, they were blended into the coffee-chocolate combo that's still enjoyed today.

> 2½ cups whole milk
>
> ¼ cup heavy cream
>
> ½ cup whole coffee beans, caffeinated or decaffeinated, preferably a dark roast coffee
>
> 3 ounces semisweet or bittersweet chocolate, chopped
>
> 2 tablespoons cocoa powder, sifted
>
> 6 large egg yolks, at room temperature
>
> ⅔ cup sugar
>
> 1 teaspoon vanilla extract
>
> ¼ teaspoon salt

1. Heat the milk and cream in a medium saucepan until small bubbles appear around the pan's inner edge. Stir in the coffee beans, cover the pan, remove it from the heat, and steep for 20 minutes.

2. Remove the beans from the milk mixture with a slotted spoon and return the pan to low heat. Stir in the chopped chocolate and cocoa powder; cook, whisking constantly, until the chocolate melts and the mixture is smooth. Set aside.

3. Beat the egg yolks and sugar in a medium bowl with a whisk or an electric mixer at medium speed until thick and pale yellow, about 2 minutes. Whisk in about a third of the chocolate milk mixture until smooth, then whisk this combined mixture back into the pan with the remaining hot chocolate mixture. Place the pan over very low heat and cook slowly, stirring constantly, until the mixture thickens slightly and coats the back of a wooden spoon, about 1 minute. Strain through a

fine-mesh sieve into a clean bowl; stir in the vanilla and salt. Refrigerate until cold, for about 4 hours, or overnight.

4. As you prepare your ice cream machine, place the mocha custard and your machine's dasher, if possible, in the freezer to make sure they're very cold, for no more than 10 minutes.

5. Freeze the custard in your ice cream machine according to the manufacturer's instructions. Serve at once—or transfer to a large container or single-serving containers and store in the freezer, tightly sealed, for up to 1 month; soften at room temperature for up to 10 minutes before serving.

Customize it!
Mix ²/₃ cup of any of the following, or any combination of the following, into the machine when the gelato's almost firm, or into the finished gelato as you mound it into a storage container: chocolate-covered espresso beans, chocolate-covered peanuts, chocolate-covered raisins, chopped caramels, chopped chocolate caramels, chopped chocolate-covered pretzels, chopped KitKat bars, chopped toasted almonds, chopped toasted hazelnuts, chopped toasted pecans, chopped toasted walnuts, chopped toffee candy bars, cocoa nibs, crumbled chocolate-covered graham crackers, M&M's Mini Baking Bits, milk chocolate chips, mini marshmallows, Reese's Pieces, semisweet chocolate chips, shaved semisweet or bittersweet chocolate, or white chocolate chips.

Orange Gelato

Makes about 1 quart (can be doubled for half-gallon machines)

Orange juice concentrate gives this creamy gelato an intense pop—and assures that the custard won't curdle. Because of the extra liquid, we'd upped the cream for more body.

> **6 large egg yolks, at room temperature**
> **⅔ cup sugar**
> **1½ cups whole milk**
> **½ cup cream**
> **One 12-ounce can orange juice concentrate, thawed to room temperature**
> **¼ teaspoon salt**

1. Beat the egg yolks and sugar in a medium bowl with a whisk or an electric mixer at medium speed until the mixture makes satiny ribbons when drizzled from the whisk or the beaters, about 3 minutes. Set aside.

2. Heat the milk and cream in a medium saucepan set over medium heat until small bubbles pop up along the pan's inner rim. Adjust the heat to maintain this just-below-a-boil temperature.

3. Whisk about half of the hot milk mixture into the egg-yolk mixture until smooth, then whisk this combined mixture back into the remaining hot milk mixture in the pan. Instantly reduce the heat to very low—or use a second burner just now set on low if you're working on an electric stove. Cook slowly, stirring nonstop, until the mixture begins to get foamy, has a few puffs of steam rising from its surface, and can coat the back of a wooden spoon, about 2 minutes. Remove the pan from the heat and stir in the orange juice concentrate. Strain through a fine-mesh sieve into a clean bowl; stir in the salt. Refrigerate until cold, for about 4 hours, or overnight.

4. Just before you make the orange gelato, place the custard and your ice cream machine's dasher, if possible, in the freezer to assure they're both quite cold, for no more than 10 minutes.

5. Freeze the custard in your ice cream machine according to the manufacturer's instructions. Serve at once—or scoop into a large container or several smaller ones,
   seal tightly, and store in the freezer for up to 1 month; soften at room temperature
   for up to 10 minutes before serving.

Orange Cheesecake Gelato   Mix ¼ cup no-bake cheesecake mix into the custard with the salt.

Orange Chip Gelato   Reduce the milk to 1¼ cups. Use 1 additional large egg
yolk. Add ¼ cup white crème de cacao with the salt. Add ⅔ cup semisweet or mini
chocolate chips to the machine when the gelato is almost firm, or stir into the finished
gelato as it's transferred to a large container.

Orange Mint Gelato   Add ½ teaspoon mint extract with the salt.

Orange Pecan Coconut Gelato   Add ½ cup chopped toasted pecans and ½ cup
toasted sweetened shredded coconut to the machine when the gelato's almost firm, or
stir into the finished gelato as it's placed in a large storage container.

Orange Pineapple Gelato   Reduce the orange juice concentrate to one
6-ounce can; add one 6-ounce can pineapple juice concentrate with the remaining orange juice concentrate.

Orange Vanilla Gelato   Add 2 teaspoons vanilla extract with the salt. Mix
⅔ cup crumbled vanilla wafer cookies or vanilla cream sandwich cookies into the machine when the gelato is almost firm, or into the finished gelato as it's transferred or
dispensed into a large container.

PEACH GELATO

Makes about 1 quart (can be doubled for half-gallon machines)

Ripe peaches are wonderfully juicy, but they unfortunately yield icy gelato. We've used all-fruit peach spread, plus fewer egg yolks, as well as a ripe peach—all for that peaches-and-cream taste.

> **One 10-ounce jar all-fruit peach spread**
> **1 large ripe peach, pitted and chopped (about 1 cup)**
> **½ teaspoon lemon juice**
> **¼ teaspoon salt**
> **3 large egg yolks, at room temperature**
> **⅓ cup sugar**
> **1¾ cups whole milk**
> **¼ cup heavy cream**

1. Place the all-fruit spread and the chopped peach in a food processor fitted with the chopping blade or a wide-canister blender. Pulse a few times, just to blend, then process or blend until smooth. Place this mixture in a fine-mesh sieve set over a small bowl; press gently against the mesh with the back of a wooden spoon to remove any peach skin or hard bits. You should end up with about 1½ cups peach puree. Stir in the lemon juice and salt; set aside.

2. Beat the egg yolks and sugar in a medium bowl with a whisk or an electric mixer at medium speed until thick and pale yellow, about 2 minutes. Set aside.

3. Heat the milk and cream in a medium saucepan over medium heat until tiny bubbles line the pan's inner rim. Do not boil.

4. Whisk about half of the hot milk mixture into the egg-yolk mixture until smooth, then whisk this combined mixture back into the pan with the remaining hot milk mixture. Immediately reduce the heat to very low—if you're using an electric stove, place the pan over an unused burner just now set on low. Cook

slowly, stirring all the while, until the mixture thickens to the consistency of melted ice cream and can coat the back of a wooden spoon, about 6 minutes. Strain through a clean fine-mesh strainer into a clean bowl; stir in the reserved peach puree. Refrigerate until cold, for about 4 hours, or overnight.

5. As you prepare your ice cream machine, place the peach custard and your machine's dasher, if possible, in the freezer, just to make sure they're cold, for no more than 10 minutes.

6. Freeze the custard in your ice cream machine according to your manufacturer's instructions. Serve at once—or transfer to a large container or several smaller ones, seal tightly, and store in the freezer for up to 1 month; soften at room temperature for up to 10 minutes before serving.

Peach Ginger Gelato   Stir ¼ cup chopped crystallized ginger into the chilled custard before it's frozen in the machine. Add ⅔ cup crumbled gingersnap cookies to the machine just before the gelato's ready, or stir them into firmed-up gelato as it's placed in a storage container.

Peach Honey Gelato   Substitute honey for the sugar.

Peach Melba Gelato   Soften 1 cup purchased raspberry jam in a small saucepan set over low heat, stirring constantly. Cool for 5 minutes. Layer this softened jam into the container with the gelato as you transfer it there for storage.

Peach Pie Gelato   Add ½ teaspoon ground cinnamon and ¼ teaspoon grated nutmeg with the salt. Add ⅔ cup crumbled graham cracker cookies to the machine just before the gelato firms up, or stir into the finished gelato as it's scooped into a storage container.

Peach Walnut Crisp Gelato   Mix ½ cup crumbled oatmeal cookies and ½ cup chopped walnuts into the machine just before the gelato's firm, or stir into the finished gelato as it's transferred to a storage container.

PEANUT BUTTER GELATO

Makes about 1 quart (can be doubled for half-gallon machines)

This creamy, luscious gelato may be just the thing when you want a treat completely over the top.

> 5 large egg yolks, at room temperature
> ¾ cup sugar
> 2½ cups whole milk
> ¼ cup heavy cream
> ⅔ cup creamy peanut butter
> 2 teaspoons vanilla extract

1. Beat the egg yolks and sugar in a medium bowl with a whisk or an electric mixer at medium speed until thin, even if grainy, and lightly colored, about 2 minutes. Set aside.

2. Heat the milk and cream in a medium saucepan set over medium heat until small bubbles appear around the pan's inner rim; do not boil but adjust the heat to maintain these bubbles.

3. Whisk about a quarter of the hot milk mixture into the egg-yolk mixture until smooth, then whisk the combined mixture back into the remaining hot milk mixture in the pan. Immediately reduce the heat to very low—if you're using an electric stove, move the pan to a second burner just now set on low. Cook slowly, stirring all the while, until the mixture thickens slightly, about like smooth, very wet pancake batter, and can coat the back of a wooden spoon, about 6 minutes. Remove from the heat and whisk in the peanut butter until smooth. Strain through a fine-mesh sieve into a clean bowl; stir in the vanilla. Refrigerate until cold, for about 4 hours, or overnight.

4. As you prepare your ice cream machine, place the custard and your machine's dasher, if possible, in the freezer to assure they're both cold, for no more than 10 minutes.

5. Freeze the custard in your ice cream machine according to your manufacturer's instructions. Serve at once—or scoop into a large container or several smaller ones, seal well, and store in the freezer for up to 1 month; soften at room temperature for up to 10 minutes before serving.

Customize it!

Substitute any of the following for the peanut butter: almond butter, cashew butter, chocolate hazelnut spread such as Nutella, hazelnut butter, or walnut butter.

And/or add ²/₃ cup of one of the following, or any combination of the following, to the machine just before the gelato sets, or mix into the finished gelato as it's placed in a container for storage: chocolate sprinkles, chocolate-covered peanuts, chocolate-covered raisins, crumbled graham crackers, crumbled peanut butter cream sandwich cookies, dried cherries, dried cranberries, M&M's Mini Baking Bits, milk chocolate chips, Reese's Pieces, or semisweet chocolate chips.

And/or layer 1 cup of any of the following into the storage container as the gelato is spooned or dispensed into it, making three or four thin layers between the gelato: purchased butterscotch ice cream sauce, chocolate ice cream sauce, marshmallow ice cream topping, strawberry ice cream sauce, or wet walnut ice cream topping.

PECAN GELATO

Makes about 1 quart (can be doubled for half-gallon machines)

Although pecans are indigenous to North America, not Italian in the least, they make a superb gelato. Serve a scoop with some honey or maple syrup drizzled on top, or alongside a slice of pound cake.

> **2 cups pecan halves**
> **3 cups whole milk, or more as necessary**
> **4 large egg yolks, at room temperature**
> **⅓ cup packed light brown sugar**
> **⅓ cup granulated sugar**
> **½ cup heavy cream**
> **½ teaspoon vanilla extract**
> **¼ teaspoon salt**

1. Position a rack in the center of the oven and preheat the oven to 350°F. Spread the pecans evenly across a large baking sheet; toast in the oven, stirring occasionally, until lightly browned and fragrant, about 5 minutes. Cool on the baking sheet for 10 minutes.

2. Place the toasted pecans and the milk in a large saucepan. Bring the mixture to a simmer over medium heat; reduce the heat and simmer at the lowest bubble for 5 minutes, stirring occasionally. Cover the pan, remove it from the heat, and steep for 20 minutes. Meanwhile, line a sieve or colander with cheesecloth and set it over a large bowl.

3. Place the pecans and milk in a large food processor fitted with the chopping blade or in a wide-canister blender. Process or blend until fairly smooth, scraping down the sides of the bowl as necessary. (See page 16 for a note on how to deal with hot liquids in a blender.) Transfer this puree to the prepared sieve and drain until almost all the liquid has leached into the bowl, about 15 minutes.

4. Gather the cheesecloth together with the nuts inside it and hold over the sieve and bowl. Squeeze gently but firmly to remove as much milk as possible. You should have about 2½ cups pecan milk; if not, add enough whole milk to make it the desired amount.

5. Beat the egg yolks and both kinds of sugar in a medium bowl with a whisk or an electric mixer at medium speed until the mixture is thick enough to make satiny ribbons when the whisk or beaters are pulled up from it, about 3 minutes. Set aside.

6. Stir the prepared pecan milk and the cream in a medium saucepan and set it over medium heat until small bubbles appear along the pan's inner rim, stirring occasionally to prevent scorching.

7. Whisk about a third of the hot pecan milk mixture into the egg-yolk mixture until smooth, then whisk this combined mixture into the remaining pecan milk mixture in the pan. Reduce the heat to very low at once—or use a second burner just now set on low if you're working on an electric stove. Cook slowly, stirring all the while, until the mixture thickens slightly, just enough to coat the back of a wooden spoon, about 5 minutes. Strain through a clean fine-mesh sieve into a clean bowl; stir in the vanilla and salt. Refrigerate until well chilled, for about 4 hours, or overnight.

8. Just before you make the pecan gelato, place the custard and your ice cream machine's dasher, if possible, in the freezer to get them very cold, for no more than 10 minutes.

9. Freeze the custard in your ice cream machine according to the manufacturer's instructions. Serve at once—or scoop into a large container or several smaller ones, seal well, and store in the freezer for up to 1 month; soften at room temperature for up to 10 minutes before serving.

Pecan Crunch Gelato Add ⅔ cup chopped candied pecans to the machine just before the gelato's ready, or stir into the finished gelato as it's placed in a storage container.

Pecan Honey Gelato Substitute ⅔ cup honey for the brown sugar and the granulated sugar.

Pecan Maple Gelato   Substitute ⅔ cup maple sugar for the brown sugar and the granulated sugar.

Pecan Pie Gelato   Add ⅔ cup crumbled graham crackers to the machine just before the gelato is firm, or stir into the finished gelato as it's placed into a storage container.

Pecan Praline Gelato   Add ⅔ cup pecan pralines to the machine just before the gelato firms up, or stir into the finished gelato as it's placed in a container for storage.

Pecan Turtle Gelato   Add ⅔ cup semisweet chocolate chips to the machine just before the gelato firms up, or stir into the finished gelato as it goes into a storage container. As it goes into that container, layer 1 cup purchased caramel sauce into the gelato, making three or four thin layers of the sauce.

PINE NUT GELATO

Makes about 1 quart (can be doubled for half-gallon machines)

Pine nuts (in Italian, *pignoli*) have a light cedar taste with a nutty richness, an elegant treat in this silky frozen custard. Store any unused nuts in the freezer.

> 1 cup pine nuts
> 2 cups whole milk
> ⅓ cup heavy cream
> 5 large egg yolks, at room temperature
> ¾ cup sugar
> ½ teaspoon vanilla extract
> ¼ teaspoon salt

1. Preheat the oven to 350°F. Spread the pine nuts evenly across a large baking sheet and toast them in the oven until lightly browned and fragrant, stirring often, about 7 minutes. Cool for 5 minutes.

2. Heat the milk and cream in a medium saucepan set over medium heat until small bubbles appear along the edges of the pan. Do not boil.

3. Place the toasted pine nuts in a food processor fitted with the chopping blade; process until fairly smooth. Add the egg yolks and the sugar; continue processing until smooth and thick.

4. With the machine running, dribble about a third of the hot milk mixture into the food processor through the open feed tube, then whisk this combined mixture into the saucepan. Instantly reduce the heat to very low—if you have an electric stove, use a burner that hasn't already been turned on. Cook slowly, stirring all the while, until the mixture is thickened to the consistency of smooth, wet pancake batter and can coat the back of a wooden spoon, about 3 minutes. Strain through a fine-mesh sieve into a medium bowl to remove any bits of scrambled egg, then stir in the vanilla and salt. Refrigerate until well chilled, for about 4 hours, or overnight.

5. Just before you make the gelato, place the custard and the dasher of your ice cream machine, if possible, in the freezer for 10 minutes to get them really cold.

6. Freeze the custard in your ice cream machine according to the manufacturer's instructions. Serve at once—or scoop into one larger container or several smaller ones, seal tightly, and store in the freezer for up to 1 month; soften at room temperature for up to 10 minutes before serving.

Pine Nut Brown Sugar Gelato   Reduce the granulated sugar to ¼ cup; add ½ cup packed light brown sugar with the remaining sugar.

Pine Nut Chip Gelato   Add ⅔ cup semisweet chocolate chips to the machine when the gelato is almost ready, or stir into the finished gelato as it's placed in a storage container.

Pine Nut Honey Gelato   Substitute honey for the sugar.

Pine Nut Raisin Gelato   Add ⅔ cup golden raisins to the machine when the gelato is almost ready, or stir into the finished gelato as it's placed in a storage container.

PISTACHIO GELATO

Makes about 1 quart (can be doubled for half-gallon machines)

Of all the nut gelati, pistachio may well be the most satisfying—probably because pistachios are rich enough to create a super-smooth custard.

> 1½ cups raw, shelled, unsalted pistachios
> 3½ cups whole milk, or more as necessary
> 4 large egg yolks, at room temperature
> ¾ cup plus 2 tablespoons sugar
> ¼ cup heavy cream
> 1 teaspoon vanilla extract
> ½ teaspoon salt, or less to taste
> 2 or 3 drops green food coloring, optional

1. Place the pistachios and milk in a large saucepan and bring the mixture to a simmer over medium-high heat. Reduce the heat and continue to simmer at the lowest bubble for 3 minutes—do not allow the mixture to roil in the pan. Cover, remove from the heat, and steep for 15 minutes. Meanwhile, line a sieve or colander with cheesecloth and set it over a large bowl.

2. Place the nuts and milk in a food processor fitted with the chopping blade or a wide-canister blender (see page 16 for a note on how to deal with hot mixtures in a blender). Process or blend until fairly smooth, scraping down the sides of the bowl as needed. You can work in batches, if necessary.

3. Pour the nut puree into the prepared sieve; drain for 10 minutes or until almost all the liquid has leached out. Gather the cheesecloth together with the nut mass inside it and hold over the sieve and bowl. Squeeze gently to remove every last drop of liquid. You should end up with about 2½ cups pistachio milk; if you don't, add enough whole milk to come up to the desired amount.

4. Beat the egg yolks and sugar in a medium bowl with a whisk or an electric mixer at medium speed until thick and pale yellow, like a grainy quick-bread batter, about 2 minutes. Set aside.

5. Mix the pistachio milk and the cream in a medium saucepan and set it over medium heat until there are tiny bubbles around the pan's inner rim, stirring occasionally to prevent scorching. Do not allow the mixture to boil.

6. Whisk about half of the hot pistachio milk mixture into the egg-yolk mixture until smooth, then beat this combined mixture back into the remaining hot pistachio milk mixture in the pan. Immediately reduce the heat to very low—or move the pan to an unused burner just now set on low if you're working on an electric stove. Cook slowly, stirring all the while, until the mixture thickens to the consistency of melted ice cream and can coat the back of a wooden spoon, about 3 minutes. Strain through a clean fine-mesh sieve into a second bowl; stir in the vanilla, salt, and food coloring, if using. Refrigerate until cold, for about 4 hours, or overnight.

7. As you prepare your ice cream machine, place the custard and your machine's dasher, if possible, in the freezer to assure they're very cold, for no more than 10 minutes.

8. Freeze the custard in your ice cream machine according to the manufacturer's instructions. Serve at once—or scoop into a larger container or several smaller ones, seal tightly, and store in the freezer for up to 1 month; soften at room temperature for up to 10 minutes before serving.

Pistachio Biscotti Gelato Add ⅔ cup crumbled biscotti to the machine when the gelato's almost ready, or stir into the finished gelato as it's placed in a storage container.

Pistachio Chip Gelato Add ⅔ cup semisweet chocolate chips to the machine when the gelato's almost ready, or stir into the finished gelato as it's placed in a storage container.

Pistachio Fudge Gelato Use 1 cup purchased chocolate sauce or softened, cooled hot fudge sauce to make three or four thin layers of sauce in the gelato as it's scooped or dispensed into a storage container.

Pumpkin Gelato

Makes about 1 quart (can be doubled for half-gallon machines)

Canned pumpkin sold in the United States is usually not pumpkin at all. The U.S. Department of Agriculture allows the more durable blue hubbard squash to be labeled as pumpkin, so most of us grew up eating squash pie, not pumpkin pie. Still, it's a taste we've come to love—no wonder few can resist pumpkin (or blue hubbard squash) gelato.

> 6 large egg yolks, at room temperature
> ½ cup packed dark brown sugar
> ¼ cup granulated sugar
> 2¼ cups whole milk
> ¼ cup heavy cream
> ¾ cup canned solid-pack pumpkin (do not use "pumpkin pie filling")
> 1 teaspoon vanilla extract
> ¼ teaspoon salt

1. Beat the egg yolks, brown sugar, and granulated sugar in a medium bowl with a whisk or an electric mixer at medium speed until thick and dark beige, but still grainy, about 2 minutes. Set aside.

2. Heat the milk and cream in a medium saucepan set over medium heat until small bubbles frizzle along the pan's inner rim. Adjust the heat so the mixture stays hot without coming to a boil.

3. Whisk about half of the hot milk mixture into the egg-yolk mixture until smooth, then whisk this combined mixture back into the pan with the remaining hot milk mixture. Whisk in the canned pumpkin. Immediately reduce the heat to very low—if you're working on an electric stove, move the pan to an unused burner just now set on low. Cook slowly, stirring constantly, until the mixture thickens to the consistency of smooth cake batter and can coat the back of a wooden spoon, about 2 minutes. Strain through a fine-mesh sieve into a clean

bowl to remove any cooked egg; stir in the vanilla and salt. Refrigerate until cold, for about 4 hours, or overnight.

4. Just before you make the gelato, place the pumpkin custard and your ice cream machine's dasher, if possible, in the freezer to shock them very cold, for no more than 10 minutes.

5. Freeze the custard in your ice cream machine according to the manufacturer's instructions. Serve at once—or scoop into a large container or several smaller ones and store in the freezer, tightly sealed, for up to 1 month; soften at room temperature for up to 10 minutes before serving.

Pumpkin Chip Gelato   Add ⅓ cup semisweet chocolate chips and ⅓ cup white chocolate chips to the machine when the gelato's almost ready, or stir into the finished gelato as it's placed in a storage container.

Pumpkin Pudding Gelato   Reduce the milk to 2 cups; add ¼ cup pineapple juice concentrate, thawed, with the vanilla. Add ½ cup mini marshmallows and ⅓ cup chopped pecans to the machine just before the gelato's firm, or stir into the finished gelato as it's put in a container for storage.

Pumpkin Rum Gelato   Reduce the milk to 2 cups. Use 1 additional large egg yolk. Stir ¼ cup dark rum, such as Myers's Dark Rum, into the chilled custard just before it's frozen in the machine.

Spiced Pumpkin Gelato   Add 1 teaspoon ground cinnamon, ½ teaspoon ground ginger, and ¼ teaspoon grated nutmeg with the vanilla.

RAISIN GELATO

Makes about 1 quart (can be doubled for half-gallon machines)

Raisin gelato (*malaga* in Italian) is a very sophisticated taste—like a big bowl of raisins and sweetened milk—perfect for adults with a lot of kid in them.

  2½ cups whole milk
  1¼ cups raisins
  ⅓ cup heavy cream
  6 large egg yolks, at room temperature
  ½ cup sugar
  ½ teaspoon vanilla extract
  ¼ teaspoon salt

1. Heat the milk, raisins, and heavy cream in a medium saucepan set over medium heat until the mixture comes to the barest simmer, just bubbles along the pan's inner rim. Cover, remove from the heat, and steep for 10 minutes.

2. Beat the egg yolks and sugar in a medium bowl with a whisk or an electric mixer at medium speed until thick and lightly colored, about 2 minutes. Set aside.

3. Place the hot raisin mixture in a wide-canister blender or a large food processor fitted with the chopping blade. Blend or process until smooth. (For a note on how to deal with hot liquids in a blender, see page 16.)

4. Whisk about a third of the hot raisin mixture into the egg-yolk mixture until fairly smooth, then transfer this mixture to a medium saucepan, set it over very low heat, and whisk in the remainder of the raisin puree. Cook slowly, stirring all the while, until the mixture begins to get foamy and can coat the back of a wooden spoon, about 5 minutes. Strain through a fine-mesh sieve into a clean bowl; stir in the vanilla and salt. Refrigerate until well chilled, for about 4 hours, or overnight.

5. Just before you make the raisin gelato, place the custard and your ice cream machine's dasher, if possible, in the freezer to make sure they're very cold, for no more than 10 minutes.

6. Freeze the custard in your ice cream machine according to the manufacturer's instructions. Serve at once—or transfer the raisin gelato to a large container or a set of individual-serving containers and store in the freezer, tightly sealed, for up to 1 month; soften at room temperature for up to 10 minutes before serving.

Prune Gelato   Substitute 6 ounces pitted prunes for the raisins.

Raisin Rum Gelato   Reduce the milk to 2¼ cups. Use 1 additional large egg yolk. Stir in ⅓ cup gold rum with the vanilla.

Shoofly Pie Gelato   Reduce the sugar to ¼ cup; add ¼ cup unsulphured molasses with the remaining sugar.

RASPBERRY GELATO

Makes about 1 quart (can be doubled for half-gallon machines)

Raspberries give this creamy gelato a spiky, tart taste, somewhat reminiscent of frozen yogurt. We've cut down on the egg yolks so that nothing can compete with the delicate taste of the berries.

> 2 cups (about 12 ounces) fresh raspberries, or 2 cups frozen raspberries (about 15 ounces), thawed
> 3 large egg yolks, at room temperature
> 1 cup sugar
> 1⅓ cups whole milk
> ½ cup heavy cream
> ¼ teaspoon salt

1. Place the berries in a fine-mesh sieve set over a small bowl and use the back of a wooden spoon to push them against the mesh, thereby removing the seeds but saving the pulp and juice. You'll need to wipe the mass gently across the mesh as it becomes denser and denser. (Alternatively, run the berries through a food mill placed over a small bowl.) Set the raspberry puree aside; discard the seeds and skins.

2. Beat the egg yolks and sugar in a medium bowl with a whisk or an electric mixer at medium speed until thick and paste-like but well emulsified, about 2 minutes. Set aside.

3. Heat the milk and cream in a medium saucepan set over medium heat, just until tiny bubbles appear around the inner rim of the pan. Adjust the heat so the mixture does not boil.

4. Whisk about half of the hot milk mixture into the egg-yolk mixture until smooth. Then whisk this combined mixture into the remaining hot milk mixture until smooth. Instantly reduce the heat to very low—if you're using an electric

stove, use a second burner just now set on low. Cook slowly, stirring constantly, until the mixture thickens slightly, like melted ice cream, but can nevertheless coat the back of a wooden spoon, about 6 minutes. Strain through a fine-mesh sieve into a clean bowl, thereby removing any bits of cooked egg. Stir in the reserved raspberry puree and salt. Refrigerate until cold, for about 4 hours, or overnight.

5. Just before making the raspberry gelato, place the custard and your ice cream machine's dasher, if possible, in the freezer, to assure they're very cold, for no more than 10 minutes.

6. Freeze the custard in your ice cream machine according to the manufacturer's instructions. Serve at once—or transfer to a large container or individual-serving containers, seal well, and store in the freezer for up to 1 month; soften at room temperature for up to 10 minutes before serving.

Customize it!

Add ²/₃ cup of any of the following, or any combination of the following, to the machine just seconds before the gelato's ready, or stir into the firmed-up gelato as it's transferred to a storage container: Cap'n Crunch or Cap'n Crunch's Crunchberry cereal, chopped dried bananas, chopped dried peaches, crumbled Girl Scout Thin Mint cookies, crumbled mint Oreo cookies, crumbled pecan Sandies cookies, cubed pitted fresh peaches, milk chocolate chips, M&M's Mini Baking Bits, mint chocolate chips, or semisweet chocolate chips.

RICE PUDDING GELATO

Makes about 1 quart (can be doubled for half-gallon machines)

Here's a traditional gelato, known in Italian ice cream shops as *riso*. The time-honored flavoring is anise, but we've left that for a variation so that ours is simply a frozen version of rice pudding. Use only Arborio rice, the short-grain variety used for risotto.

> 3½ cups whole milk
> ⅓ cup Arborio rice
> 6 large egg yolks, at room temperature
> ¾ cup sugar
> 1 teaspoon vanilla extract
> ¼ teaspoon grated nutmeg
> ¼ teaspoon salt

1. Place the milk and rice in a medium saucepan, set over medium-high heat, and bring the mixture to a simmer. Adjust the heat to maintain a very low simmer, cover the pan, and cook, stirring often to prevent sticking, until the rice is tender, about 40 minutes. Remove from the heat and let stand for 5 minutes.

2. While the rice and milk are still warm, beat the egg yolks and sugar in a medium bowl with a whisk or an electric mixer at medium speed until thick and pale yellow, about 2 minutes.

3. Whisk about a third of the hot milk and rice into the egg-yolk mixture until smooth, then whisk this combined mixture back into the pan with the remaining milk mixture. Set the pan over low heat and cook, stirring constantly, until the mixture coats the back of a wooden spoon, about 30 seconds. (You cannot strain the mixture because you would lose all the rice—so you need to make sure you cook it just long enough to set the eggs, not until they begin to scramble.) Remove from the heat and stir in the vanilla, nutmeg, and salt. Pour into a clean bowl and refrigerate until cold, for about 4 hours, or overnight.

4. As you prepare your ice cream machine, place the rice custard and the machine's dasher, if possible, in the freezer to make sure they're both very cold, for no more than 10 minutes.

5. Freeze the custard in your ice cream machine according to the manufacturer's instructions. Serve at once—or scoop into a large container or several smaller ones, seal well, and store in the freezer for up to 2 weeks; soften at room temperature for up to 10 minutes before serving.

Italian Riso Gelato Substitute ½ teaspoon anise extract for the vanilla; omit the grated nutmeg.

Customize it!

Add ⅔ cup of any of the following, or any combination of the following, to the machine just seconds before the gelato's ready, or stir into the firmed-up gelato as it's transferred to a storage container: chopped dried apricots, chopped dried figs, chopped dried pears, chopped dried pineapple, chopped pitted dates, dried blueberries, dried cherries, dried cranberries, dried currants, dried strawberries, golden raisins, or raisins.

Stracciatella Gelato

Makes about 1 quart (can be doubled for half-gallon machines)

Although often called "chocolate chip gelato" in English, stracciatella is actually made from shaved chocolate. When folded in, these shavings create the strata, or layers, that give the gelato its name. You'll need two 1-ounce squares of chocolate, or a 2-ounce chunk off a larger block. This is such a classic that any variations would just muck it up.

> **6 egg yolks, at room temperature**
> **⅔ cup sugar**
> **2½ cups whole milk**
> **⅓ cup heavy cream**
> **2 teaspoons vanilla extract**
> **¼ teaspoon salt**
> **2 ounces bittersweet or semisweet chocolate (do not use chips)**

1. Beat the egg yolks and sugar in a medium bowl with a whisk or an electric mixer at medium speed until thick like a grainy batter, about 2 minutes. Set aside.

2. Heat the milk and cream in a medium saucepan set over medium heat until tiny bubbles appear along the pan's inner rim; do not allow the mixture to boil but maintain the heat so it stays this hot.

3. Whisk about half of the hot milk mixture into the egg-yolk mixture until smooth, then whisk this combined mixture into the remaining hot milk mixture in the pan. Immediately reduce the heat to very low—if you're using an electric stove, place the pan on an unused burner set on low. Cook slowly, stirring constantly, until the mixture thickens to the consistency of smooth, wet pancake batter and can coat the back of a wooden spoon, about 7 minutes. Strain through a fine-mesh sieve into a clean bowl to remove any bits of scrambled egg; stir in the vanilla and salt. Refrigerate until cold, for about 4 hours, or overnight.

4. As you prepare your ice cream machine, place the custard and the machine's dasher, if possible, in the freezer to get them both very cold; leave them there for no more than 10 minutes.

5. Freeze the custard in your ice cream machine according to the manufacturer's instructions. While it's freezing, hold the chocolate over a bowl to catch every tiny shard and shave the chocolate with a vegetable peeler so that the uneven shavings and shards are caught in the bowl. Just when the mixture is firm and ready to be served, add the shaved chocolate to the gelato and let the machine turn it a few times—or stir in the shaved chocolate by hand. Serve at once—or scoop into a large container or several individual-serving containers, seal well, and store in the freezer for up to 1 month; soften at room temperature for up to 10 minutes before serving.

STRAWBERRY GELATO

Makes about 1 quart (can be doubled for half-gallon machines)

Strawberry gelato is one of summer's best treasures, light and fresh. In this recipe, the all-fruit spread gives you the intense taste of strawberries, and the fresh berries, their characteristic brightness.

> **6 large fresh strawberries**
> **5 large egg yolks, at room temperature**
> **½ cup sugar**
> **2 cups whole milk**
> **½ cup heavy cream**
> **One 10-ounce jar all-fruit strawberry spread**
> **¼ teaspoon salt**
> **2 or 3 drops red food coloring, optional**

1. Place the strawberries in a blender, a mini food processor, or a food processor fitted with the chopping blade; blend or process to a fine, light puree, about 30 seconds, scraping down the sides of the bowl as necessary. If you prefer no seeds, run the whole strawberries through a food mill set over a small bowl, thereby catching the pulp and juice but removing the seeds. Set aside.

2. Beat the egg yolks and sugar in a medium bowl with a whisk or an electric mixer at medium speed until thick and pale yellow, but not until the mixture makes satiny ribbons when dripped from the whisk or beaters, about 2 minutes. Set aside.

3. Heat the milk and cream in a medium saucepan set over medium heat until small bubbles form around the pan's inner rim. Do not boil but maintain this heat in the pan.

4. Whisk about half of the hot milk mixture into the egg-yolk mixture until smooth, then whisk this combined mixture back into the remaining hot milk

mixture. Immediately reduce the heat to very low; use a second burner just now set on low if you're cooking on an electric stove. Cook slowly, stirring constantly, until the mixture begins to get foamy, starts to smell eggy, and can coat the back of a wooden spoon, about 7 minutes. Strain through a fine-mesh sieve into a clean bowl; stir in the all-fruit spread, reserved strawberry puree, salt, and food coloring, if using. Refrigerate until well chilled, for at least 4 hours, or overnight.

5. While you're getting your ice cream machine ready, place the custard and your machine's dasher, if possible, in the freezer, just to assure they're very cold, for no more than 10 minutes.

6. Freeze the custard in your ice cream machine according to the manufacturer's instructions. Serve at once—or transfer to a large container or several small containers, seal tightly, and store in the freezer for up to 1 month; soften at room temperature for up to 10 minutes before serving.

Customize it!

Add ⅔ cup of any of the following, or any combination of the following, to the machine just seconds before the gelato's ready, or stir into the firmed-up gelato as it's transferred to a storage container: chopped Junior Mints, chopped peppermint-patty candies, crumbled strawberry cream wafer cookies, crushed chocolate cream sandwich cookies, granola, milk chocolate chips, mint chocolate chips, peanut butter chocolate chips, Reese's Pieces, semisweet chocolate chips, or white chocolate chips.

Torroncino Gelato

Makes about 1 quart (can be doubled for half-gallon machines)

Here's a gelato based on torrone, the Italian nougat candy made with honey and almonds. You'll first make a classic almond brittle, or nougatine, then pulverize it and fold it into a honey-laced custard.

> ¾ **cup sugar**
>
> ½ **cup honey**
>
> ½ **cup sliced almonds**
>
> 6 **large egg yolks, at room temperature**
>
> 2¾ **cups whole milk**
>
> ¼ **cup heavy cream**
>
> 1 **teaspoon almond extract**
>
> ½ **teaspoon vanilla extract**
>
> ¼ **teaspoon salt, or less to taste**

1. Line a large baking sheet with a silicone baking mat or parchment paper; set aside. Stir ¼ cup of the sugar and ¼ cup of the honey in a large skillet, preferably nonstick, until fairly smooth, then set the pan over medium-high heat. Cook undisturbed until the sugar has melted, about 1 minute. Stir in the almonds and continue cooking, stirring occasionally, until the sugar caramelizes and the almonds brown lightly, about 4 minutes. Pour the mixture out in a thin layer onto the prepared baking sheet. Cool for 1 hour at room temperature.

2. Lift the nougatine off the sheet and break it into large chunks; place them in a food processor fitted with the chopping blade and pulse until pulverized. (The recipe can be made up to this point in advance; place the pulverized candy in a plastic bag or small container, seal well, and store at room temperature in a cool, dry place for up to 2 days.)

3. Beat the remaining ½ cup of sugar and the egg yolks with a whisk or an electric mixer at medium speed until light and batter-like, even if still grainy, about 2 minutes. Set aside.

4. Heat the milk and cream in a medium saucepan set over medium heat until small bubbles dot the inside rim of the pan. Stir in the remaining ¼ cup of honey until dissolved. Do not boil.

5. Whisk about half of the hot milk mixture into the egg-yolk mixture until smooth, then whisk this combined mixture into the remaining hot milk mixture in the pan. Immediately reduce the heat to very low—if you're working on an electric stove, move the pan to a second burner just now set on low. Cook slowly, stirring constantly, until the mixture can coat the back of a wooden spoon, about 6 minutes. Strain through a fine-mesh sieve into a clean bowl; stir in the almond extract, vanilla, and salt. Refrigerate until cold, for at least 4 hours, or overnight.

6. As you prepare your ice cream machine, place the custard and the machine's dasher, if possible, in the freezer to chill them really well, for no more than 10 minutes.

7. Freeze the custard in your ice cream machine according to your manufacturer's instructions. Just as the gelato firms up in the machine, pour in the pulverized nougatine candy, letting the dasher mix it in for the final few turns—or stir in the pulverized candy by hand until evenly distributed. Serve at once—or scoop into a large container or several individual-serving containers, seal well, and store in your refrigerator's freezer for up to 1 month. Because of the large amount of sugar, this gelato will not harden in the freezer.

   To simplify the recipe, forego making the nougatine and use 6 ounces purchased almond brittle, ground up in the food processor.

   Or substitute 6 ounces cashew brittle, peanut brittle, or sesame brittle for the almond brittle.

VANILLA GELATO

Makes about 1 quart (can be doubled for half-gallon machines)

The simplest things in life are often the best. Use only pure vanilla extract for this rich but otherwise unadorned extravagance.

> **7 large egg yolks, at room temperature**
> **½ cup plus 2 tablespoons sugar**
> **2¾ cups whole milk**
> **¼ cup heavy cream**
> **2 tablespoons vanilla extract**
> **¼ teaspoon salt**

1. Beat the egg yolks and sugar in a medium bowl with a whisk or an electric mixer at medium speed until thick and pale lemony yellow but still gritty, about 2 minutes. Set aside.

2. Heat the milk and cream in a medium saucepan until small bubbles pop up along the pan's inner rim; adjust the heat to keep the mixture very hot but do not boil.

3. Whisk about a quarter of the hot milk mixture into the egg-yolk mixture until smooth, then whisk this combined mixture back into the saucepan with the remaining hot milk mixture. Immediately reduce the heat to very low—if you're using an electric stove, move the pan to a second burner just now set on low. Cook slowly, stirring all the while, until the mixture thickens to the consistency of smooth, very wet cake batter and can coat the back of a wooden spoon, about 7 minutes. Strain through a fine-mesh sieve into a clean bowl to remove any extraneous bits of cooked egg; stir in the vanilla and salt. Refrigerate until cold, for at least 4 hours, or overnight.

4. Just before you make the gelato, place the vanilla custard and your ice cream machine's dasher, if possible, in the freezer, just to assure they're very cold, for no more than 10 minutes.

5. Freeze the custard in your ice cream machine according to the manufacturer's instructions. Serve at once—or transfer to a large container or several individual-serving containers and store in the freezer, tightly sealed, for up to 1 month; soften at room temperature for up to 10 minutes before serving.

Customize it!

To make a swirl gelato, use 1 cup of any of the following to create thin ribbons in the gelato as it is spooned or dispensed into a storage container: softened and cooled jam, softened and cooled marmalade, butterscotch ice cream topping, caramel sauce, chocolate ice cream sauce, chocolate mocha ice cream topping, dulce de leche ice cream topping, marshmallow sauce, pineapple sauce, softened and cooled hot fudge sauce, strawberry ice cream sauce, or wet walnut ice cream topping.

To make a chip gelato, add ⅔ cup of any of the following to the machine just seconds before the gelato's ready, or stir into the firmed-up gelato as it's transferred to a storage container: butterscotch chips, cocoa nibs, milk chocolate chips, mint chocolate chips, peanut butter chips, semisweet chocolate chips, or white chocolate chips.

To make a candy gelato, add ⅔ cup of any of the following to the machine just seconds before the gelato's ready, or stir into the firmed-up gelato as it's transferred to a storage container: any chopped candy bar, candy corn, chocolate-covered espresso beans, chocolate-covered raisins, chopped caramels, chopped honey candies, chopped Jordan almonds, chopped licorice ropes, chopped chocolate mint sandwich cookies, chopped small gumballs, chopped Tootsie Rolls, gummy bears or other chopped gummy candies (not gummy sours!), Heath Bits, jelly beans, malted milk balls, mini M&M's, nonpareils, Reese's Pieces, Skittles, or ice cream sprinkles.

WALNUT GELATO

Makes about 1 quart (can be doubled for half-gallon machines)

Walnuts are one of those "super foods"—they have more omega-3 than any nut and may even make arteries supple again. But then, you're probably not eating walnut gelato for health reasons. Go hog wild and serve it with chocolate sauce or alongside a slice of pound cake.

> 2 cups walnut halves
> 3½ cups whole milk, or more as necessary
> 4 large egg yolks, at room temperature
> ½ cup packed light brown sugar
> ¼ cup granulated sugar
> ¼ cup heavy cream
> 1 teaspoon vanilla extract
> ¼ teaspoon salt

1. Position a rack in the center of the oven and preheat the oven to 350°F. Spread the walnut halves evenly across a large baking sheet and toast in the oven until lightly browned but very fragrant, stirring once in a while, about 6 minutes. Cool on the baking sheet for 5 minutes.

2. Place the nuts in a large saucepan with the milk. Set the pan over medium-high heat and bring to a simmer, stirring occasionally. Adjust the heat so the mixture slowly simmers for 5 minutes. Remove the pan from the heat, cover, and steep for 15 minutes. Meanwhile, line a sieve or a colander with cheesecloth and set it over a large bowl.

3. Place the nut mixture in a food processor fitted with the chopping blade or a wide-canister blender. Process or blend until fairly smooth. (See page 16 for a note about how to deal with hot liquids in a blender.) Transfer this walnut puree to the prepared sieve; set aside until almost all the liquid has seeped into the bowl, about 15 minutes.

4. Gather the cheesecloth together so that the nut mass is held tightly in it and hold it over the sieve and bowl. Squeeze gently to remove as much of the nut milk as you can. In the end, you should have about 2½ cups walnut milk; if not, add enough whole milk to bring the mixture up to the desired amount.

5. Mash the egg yolks and both kinds of sugar together in a medium bowl with the back of a wooden spoon until they become a grainy paste, then beat with an electric mixer at medium speed until pale yellow but still not smooth, about 2 minutes. Set aside.

6. Heat the walnut milk and cream in a medium saucepan set over medium heat just until the tiniest bubbles pop up along the pan's inner rim. Do not allow the mixture to boil.

7. Whisk about a third of the hot walnut milk mixture into the egg-yolk mixture until smooth. Whisk this combined mixture into the remaining walnut milk mixture until smooth. Reduce the heat to very low—or if you're using an electric stove, move the pan to a second burner just now turned on low. Cook slowly, stirring constantly, until the mixture rises slightly in the pan and thickens enough to coat the back of a wooden spoon, about 4 minutes. Strain through a fine-mesh sieve into a clean bowl; stir in the vanilla and salt. Refrigerate until cold, for about 4 hours, or overnight.

8. As you prepare your ice cream machine, place the walnut custard and the machine's dasher, if possible, in the freezer to get them both very cold; leave them there no more than 10 minutes.

9. Freeze the custard in your ice cream machine according to the manufacturer's instructions. Serve at once—or scoop into a large container or several smaller ones and store in the freezer, tightly sealed, for up to 1 month; soften at room temperature for up to 10 minutes before serving.

Walnut Caramel Swirl Gelato Use 1 cup purchased caramel ice cream topping to create ribbons in the gelato as it's put into a container for storage.

Walnut Fudge Swirl Gelato Use 1 cup softened, purchased hot fudge sauce to create ribbons in the gelato as it's put into a container for storage.

Walnut Mocha Chip Gelato Add 1 tablespoon instant espresso powder to the milk when you let it steep with the nuts. Add ⅔ cup semisweet chocolate chips to the machine when the gelato is just about ready, or stir into the finished gelato as it's put into a storage container.

Walnut Oatmeal Crunch Gelato Add ⅔ cup crumbled oatmeal cookies or purchased granola to the machine when the gelato is just about ready, or stir into the finished gelato as it's put into a storage container.

WHITE CHOCOLATE GELATO

Makes about 1 quart (can be doubled for half-gallon machines)

Purists remind us that white chocolate isn't chocolate at all since it has no cocoa solids, just cocoa butter. But the squinty-eyed too often miss out on real pleasures. The delicate taste of white chocolate fades over time, so this gelato is best the moment it's frozen. Look for white chocolate made without hydrogenated oil.

> 5 large egg yolks, at room temperature
> ⅓ cup sugar
> 2¼ cups whole milk
> ⅓ cup heavy cream
> 8 ounces white chocolate, chopped
> ½ teaspoon vanilla extract (use "uncolored" vanilla extract, if possible)
> ¼ teaspoon salt

1. Beat the egg yolks and sugar in a medium bowl with a whisk or an electric mixer at medium speed until the consistency of a very grainy quick-bread batter, about 2 minutes. Set aside.

2. Heat the milk and cream in a medium saucepan set over medium heat until tiny bubbles pop up around the pan's inner rim. Do not boil.

3. Whisk about a third of the hot milk mixture into the egg-yolk mixture until smooth, then whisk this combined mixture back into the pan with the remaining hot milk mixture. Immediately turn down the heat to very low—if you're using an electric stove, move the pan to a second burner just now set on low. Cook slowly, stirring constantly, until the mixture thickens to the consistency of very wet, loose cake batter and can coat the back of a wooden spoon, about 5 minutes. Remove the pan from the heat and stir in the white chocolate, vanilla, and salt until smooth. Strain through a fine-mesh sieve into a clean bowl to remove any bits of scrambled egg. Refrigerate until cold, for at least 4 hours, or overnight.

4. As you prepare your ice cream machine, place the white chocolate custard and the machine's dasher, if possible, in the freezer to assure they're very cold, for no more than 10 minutes.

5. Freeze the custard in your ice cream machine according to the manufacturer's instructions. Serve at once—or scoop into a large container or several that are good for individual servings, seal tightly, and store in the freezer for no more than 3 days; soften at room temperature for up to 10 minutes before serving.

White Chocolate Raspberry Swirl Gelato   Soften 1 cup raspberry jam in a small saucepan set over low heat, stirring constantly, for about 2 minutes. Set aside to cool for 5 minutes. Use this jam to make ribbons in the gelato as it's put in a storage container, making three or four thin strips between layers of gelato.

Customize it!
Add ⅔ cup of any of the following, or any combination of the following, to the machine just seconds before the gelato's ready, or stir into the firmed-up gelato as it's transferred to a storage container: chopped dried figs, chopped hazelnuts, chopped walnuts, dried blueberries, dried cherries, dried cranberries, dried strawberries, or peanut butter chips.

Sherbet

A mélange of milk and fruit, sherbet probably has the longest culinary history of any dessert in this book, an ancestral derivation from refreshing drinks served across the blazingly hot Middle East: *sharâb* (Arabic for an alcoholic cold fruit drink) or *sharbât* (for the nonalcoholic version). These were brought to European tables via alliances with the Ottoman Empire.

Originally, the sherbet-like drinks may have been royal treats, fruit juice poured over ice or snow trekked down from the mountains. However, when sherbets passed into Europe, they morphed into concoctions suitable for Western kitchens and tastes—and thus became *sorbetto* in Italian, *sorbet* in French, and *sherbet* in English. Early on, none of these had milk in the mix. The sherbet offered at Delmonico's in New York City in the 1860s was a citrus-and-wine sorbet served in cups made entirely of ice. In both American and British usage throughout the nineteenth century, *sorbet* and *sherbet* were interchangeable.

The twentieth century has proven the great laboratory for food. Slowly, sherbet split off from sorbet to became its own treat, thanks to two additions, probably the results of the growing demand for ice cream and the palate-shifting in the West toward silkier desserts. First, sherbet is now made with milk, which enriches it considerably. Still, it's not ice milk: the ratio of fruit to milk is much higher. Call it a fruity dessert more than a creamy one.

The second addition is some sort of thickener, usually gelatin, which improves the texture by allowing more air to be whipped into the base as it freezes. (To put it another way, gelatin increases the mixture's overrun—see page 4.) This thickener remains somewhat controversial: some chefs insist on it; others decry it. We've put gelatin in the icier sherbets, particularly those with citrus fruits, so they would have a smoother consistency.

An alternative to gelatin is corn syrup; it gives the resulting dessert a silky finish without much added air. We've included it where we feel the texture needs softening, as in the Raspberry Sherbet and the Lychee Sherbet. Still, some sherbets, like Blueberry, we've left alone—no gelatin or corn syrup at all, just milk and fruit puree—because we thought the taste of the fruit was masked with these modern conveniences.

Finally, one concession: a few fruits—papaya and pineapple among them—have digestive enzymes that both curdle milk and impede the action of gelatin. In these cases, we've used canned fruits because the enzyme is neutralized in the canning process.

Sherbet always works best with tangy fruits—citrus, berries, and tropical fruits. What's important is the zip, never cloying or heavy. In the end, we held each recipe to the same criterion: Would it take the bead off a summer day?

ABOUT MIX-INS AND ADDITIONS

Mix-ins are often herbal—mint, of course, but also thyme, rosemary, basil, and tarragon. While they're unusual, don't neglect these fresh herbs in sherbet: they give the mixture a sophisticated flavor beyond the norm. Because sherbet should be light and zippy, we've avoided chocolate chips, crumbled cookies, purchased cookie dough, and the like. In fact, we've avoided anything crunchy at all—the point here is the smooth, velvety taste.

FIVE TIPS FOR SHERBET SUCCESS

1. In these sherbet recipes, never boil the milk, or even bring it to a simmer. Heat it just to the point where you might drink it before bed on a sleepless night—a few puffs of steam, perhaps, but no bubbles along the pan's inner edge. The goal is to dissolve the sugar and gelatin before adding the fruit puree, not to change the composition of the components. Also, heat only as much milk as the recipe asks you to. The rest, kept out on the counter at room temperature, will be used to cool the warm liquids when they're blended together.

2. Gelatin is sold in two forms: granulated in ¼-ounce packets and in thin sheets, sometimes called "leaf gelatin." We only call for the former, a supermarket staple. A ¼-ounce packet (usually sold four to the box) contains about 1 tablespoon of gelatin. All these recipes call for less, usually 1 or 2 teaspoons, just enough to give the sherbet some body. It must first be softened in cool water, then dissolved in a warm liquid. Do not allow the liquid to simmer at this point—the gelatin will break down and turn stringy. Store unused gelatin, tightly wrapped, in a cool, dark place.

3. Chill the unfrozen sherbet mixture in your refrigerator before freezing it in your ice cream machine, usually for about 4 hours, or overnight. This will ensure that the fruit taste has deepened in the milk.

4. Citrus fruits can cause milk to curdle. Actually, it's nothing to fear—it allows the sour, zippier taste of real sherbet to come through. But there can be unsightly curds. To avoid them, puree the mixture in a blender before chilling. Should it turn lumpy as it chills, give it another whir to smooth it out before freezing.

5. Sherbets are best eaten soft. Those made without gelatin, if stored in your freezer, should sit out at room temperature for 5 minutes before serving. Those made with gelatin can be eaten straight out of the freezer since gelatin automatically increases the "whipability" and the resulting sherbet will never fully harden.

Apricot Sherbet

Makes about 1 quart (can be doubled for half-gallon machines)

Serve this cooling sherbet with purchased chocolate chip biscotti or amaretti, Italian cookies made from a bitter almond paste or (more authentically) ground apricot pits.

> One 15¼-ounce can pitted apricot halves in heavy syrup
> 1 tablespoon lemon juice
> ¼ teaspoon salt
> 2¼ cups whole milk
> ½ cup sugar

1. Place the apricot halves and their syrup in a large blender; blend until smooth. Add the lemon juice and salt; blend well and set aside.

2. Warm 1¼ cups of the milk in a medium saucepan set over low heat. Stir in the sugar until dissolved; cool for 5 minutes. Pour this mixture into the blender with the apricot puree. Add the remaining 1 cup milk and blend until fairly smooth, scraping down the sides of the canister as necessary. Strain through a fine-mesh sieve into a medium bowl; refrigerate until cold, for at least 4 hours, or overnight.

3. Freeze in your ice cream machine according to the manufacturer's instructions. Serve at once—or spoon into a large container, seal well, and store in the freezer for up to 1 month; soften at room temperature for 5 minutes before serving.

Customize it!
You can add any of the following to the blender with the remaining 1 cup of milk: 2 tablespoons apricot brandy or Southern Comfort, 2 tablespoons chopped fresh mint leaves, 1 tablespoon chopped fresh rosemary, 1 tablespoon chopped fresh thyme, 2 teaspoons vanilla extract, 1 teaspoon rum extract, or ½ teaspoon almond extract.

BLUEBERRY SHERBET

Makes about 1 quart (can be doubled for half-gallon machines)

This simple treat is perhaps the most refreshing sherbet in the book—it was a hit every time we took it somewhere when we were testing recipes. It's worthy of your best dessert wine.

> 1½ cups fresh blueberries (about 12 ounces)
> 1¾ cups whole milk
> 2 teaspoons lemon juice
> ¼ teaspoon salt
> ⅔ cup sugar

1. Place the blueberries and ½ cup of the milk in a large blender; blend until fairly smooth, scraping down the sides of the canister as necessary. Blend in the lemon juice and salt; set aside.

2. Warm the remaining 1¼ cups of milk in a medium saucepan over low heat. Stir in the sugar until dissolved; cool for 5 minutes. Pour into the blender with the blueberry puree; blend until smooth. Strain through a fine-mesh sieve into a medium bowl; refrigerate until well chilled, for at least 4 hours, or overnight.

3. Freeze in your ice cream machine according to the manufacturer's instructions. Serve at once—or scoop into a large container, seal well, and store in the freezer for up to 1 month; soften at room temperature for 5 minutes before serving.

Customize it!

Add any of the following to the blender with the blueberry puree: 1 peeled ripe banana, 2 tablespoons gold rum, 1 tablespoon chopped fresh mint leaves, 1 tablespoon chopped fresh thyme, 2 teaspoons finely grated orange zest, 2 teaspoons vanilla extract, ½ teaspoon ground cinnamon, or ¼ teaspoon grated nutmeg.

And/or reduce the milk to 1 cup and mix ¾ cup buttermilk with the remaining milk before proceeding with the recipe.

CANTALOUPE SHERBET

Makes about 1 quart (can be doubled for half-gallon machines)

You see people picking out cantaloupes in the supermarket—all that rapping, tapping, and pressing—and you have to wonder what they're doing. There's really only one way to tell: if it doesn't smell like a cantaloupe, it won't taste like one.

> 1 teaspoon unflavored gelatin
> 1 tablespoon cool water
> 1 ripe medium cantaloupe, cut into wedges, seeds and rind removed
> ¼ teaspoon salt
> 2 cups whole milk
> ⅔ cup sugar

1. Sprinkle the gelatin over the water in a small bowl or teacup; set aside to soften for 5 minutes.

2. Chop the cantaloupe flesh, reserving any juice. Place the chunks, juice, and salt in a blender. Blend until smooth, scraping down the sides of the canister as necessary. Set aside.

3. Warm 1 cup of the milk in a small saucepan over low heat. Stir in the sugar until dissolved. Reduce the heat to very low and stir in the gelatin mixture, just until dissolved, for no more than 20 seconds. Do not simmer.

4. Pour the warm milk mixture and the remaining 1 cup milk into the blender with the cantaloupe puree; blend until smooth. (For a note about how to deal with hot things in a blender, see page 16.) Strain through a fine-mesh sieve into a medium bowl. Refrigerate until cold, for at least 4 hours, or overnight.

5. Freeze in your ice cream machine according to the manufacturer's instructions. Serve at once—or transfer to a separate container, seal well, and store in the freezer for up to 1 month.

Honeydew Sherbet Substitute a ripe medium honeydew melon for the cantaloupe.

Customize it!
Add any of the following to the blender with the cantaloupe puree: 2 tablespoons chopped fresh basil leaves, 2 tablespoons chopped fresh mint leaves, 1 teaspoon lemon extract, 1 teaspoon ground ginger, or ½ teaspoon Tabasco sauce (or to taste).

And/or reduce the total milk used to 1 cup; heat this amount as directed in step 3. Add 1 cup coconut milk to the blender with the cantaloupe puree.

Coconut Sherbet

Makes about 1 quart (can be doubled for half-gallon machines)

Thick and smooth, this coconut sorbet can also be made with light coconut milk, although the resulting sherbet will be icier. Stir either kind of coconut milk so that any solids reincorporate into the liquid before you add it to the milk.

> 1 teaspoon unflavored gelatin
> 1 tablespoon cool water
> One 13½-ounce can unsweetened coconut milk, or light coconut milk
> (1¾ cups)
> 1½ cups whole milk
> ¾ cup sugar
> ⅛ teaspoon salt

1. Sprinkle the gelatin over the water in a small bowl or teacup; set aside to soften for 5 minutes.

2. Warm the coconut milk and milk in a medium saucepan set over low heat. Stir in the sugar and salt until dissolved, about 15 seconds. Reduce the heat to very low and stir in the gelatin mixture until dissolved. Transfer to a bowl; refrigerate until cold, whisking occasionally to prevent the coconut fat from lumping, for about 4 hours, or overnight.

3. Freeze in your ice cream machine according to the manufacturer's instructions. Serve at once—or transfer to a container and store in the freezer, tightly sealed, for up to 1 month.

Customize it!
Stir in any of the following with the gelatin mixture: ¼ cup limeade concentrate, thawed; ¼ cup pineapple juice concentrate, thawed; ¼ cup raspberry juice concentrate, thawed; ¼ cup cherry syrup; 3 tablespoons white rum, gold rum, or coconut rum; or 1 teaspoon banana extract.

GRAPEFRUIT SHERBET

Makes about 1 quart (can be doubled for half-gallon machines)

Grapefruits are so flavorful, they stand up well in this refreshing sherbet, perfect after a barbecue meal alongside a bowl of fresh berries or as a winter perk-up after a rich stew.

> **2 large grapefruits**
> **1¼ cups whole milk**
> **1 cup sugar**
> **¼ teaspoon salt**

1. Cut about ¼ inch off the bottom of each grapefruit. Stand them flat on your cutting board. Use a sharp knife to remove the rind and pith, slicing along the curve of the grapefruit's surface and revealing the pink flesh inside. Take care not to slice off too much of the fruit; reserve any juice that collects on your cutting board. Cut the flesh away from the inner membrane. Discard the rind, pith, and any seeds; chop the grapefruit flesh into chunks. Place these chunks and any reserved juice in a large blender or a food processor fitted with the chopping blade; blend or process until smooth, scraping down the sides of the bowl as necessary. Strain through a fine-mesh sieve into a medium bowl, pushing lightly against the solids with the back of a wooden spoon to remove as much juice and pulp as possible; discard the fleshy solids and set the strained puree aside.

2. Warm the milk in a medium saucepan over low heat. Stir in the sugar and salt until dissolved. Clean the blender, if you've used it; then pour this milk mixture into the canister. Add the grapefruit puree and blend until smooth. (For a note about dealing with hot things in a blender, see page 16.) Strain through a fine-mesh sieve into a clean bowl; refrigerate until cold, for at least 4 hours, or overnight.

3. Freeze in your ice cream machine according to the manufacturer's instructions. (If the mixture has curdled, blend again before freezing.) Serve at once—or scoop

into a large container, seal tightly, and store in the freezer for up to 1 month; soften at room temperature for 5 minutes before serving.

Customize it!
Add any of the following to the blender with the grapefruit puree: ¼ cup Campari, 2 tablespoons caramel syrup, 2 tablespoons strawberry syrup, 2 tablespoons vanilla syrup, 2 tablespoons chopped fresh mint leaves, 1 tablespoon chopped fresh thyme, or 1 tablespoon chopped fresh tarragon leaves.

KUMQUAT SHERBET

Makes a little less than 1 quart (can be doubled for half-gallon machines)

Kumquats are so sour that you need look no further than this tart sherbet for a great perk-up after any big meal, from Memorial Day to Thanksgiving dinner.

1 cup sugar
1 cup water
2 cups kumquats (about 12 ounces), stems removed
1 cup whole milk

1. Stir the sugar and water in a medium saucepan set over medium-high heat until the sugar dissolves. Add the kumquats and bring to a simmer. Cover, reduce the heat, and simmer until the kumquats are soft, about 10 minutes.

2. Remove the kumquats with a slotted spoon and place them in the canister of a large blender. Set aside.

3. Pour the milk into the saucepan with the sugar syrup. Bring to a simmer and boil lightly for 3 minutes, stirring frequently. Remove the pan from the heat and cool for 10 minutes.

4. Pour the milk into the blender with the kumquats; blend until smooth. Strain through a fine-mesh sieve into a medium bowl, pressing against the solids with the back of a wooden spoon to release as much liquid as possible. Discard the solids and refrigerate the milk mixture until cold, for at least 4 hours, or overnight.

5. Whisk the kumquat mixture, then freeze it in your ice cream machine according to the manufacturer's instructions. Serve at once—or scoop into a large container, seal tightly, and store in the freezer for up to 1 month; soften at room temperature for 5 minutes before serving.

Customize it!
Add 1 teaspoon orange flower water or rose water to the blender with the kumquats.

LEMON SHERBET

Makes about 1 quart (can be doubled for half-gallon machines)

Here's the easiest sherbet in the book, a no-cook refresher. If you want a classic lemon sherbet, see the variation under Lime Sherbet (page 117).

> **One 12-ounce can lemonade concentrate, thawed**
> **One 7½-ounce jar Marshmallow Fluff or Marshmallow Cream**
> **1 cup water**

1. Place all the ingredients in a large blender; blend until smooth. Transfer to a medium bowl and refrigerate until cold, for at least 4 hours, or overnight.

2. Freeze in your ice cream machine according to the manufacturer's instructions. Serve at once—or scoop into a large container, seal tightly, and store in the freezer for up to 1 month.

Customize it!
Substitute a 12-ounce can of any of the following, thawed, for the lemonade concentrate: Concord grape juice concentrate, cranberry juice concentrate, frozen daiquiri mix, grapefruit juice concentrate, limeade concentrate, pineapple juice concentrate, raspberry juice concentrate, raspberry-lemonade concentrate, or any tart juice concentrate.

LIME SHERBET

Makes about 1 quart (can be doubled for half-gallon machines)

To get the most juice out of limes, keep them at room temperature. Before cutting them, roll them along your counter, pressing down gently with your palm, to break up some of the juice sacks in the pulp.

> **1 teaspoon unflavored gelatin**
> **1 tablespoon cool water**
> **3 cups whole milk**
> **1 cup sugar**
> **¼ teaspoon salt**
> **⅔ cup lime juice, strained to include no pulp**

1. Sprinkle the gelatin over the water in a small bowl or a teacup; set aside to soften for 5 minutes.

2. Warm 1½ cups of the milk in a medium saucepan set over low heat. Stir in the sugar and salt until dissolved. Reduce the heat to very low and stir in the gelatin mixture until smooth, for no more than 20 seconds. Do not allow the mixture to simmer.

3. Pour the mixture into a large blender. Add the remaining 1½ cups milk and the lime juice. Blend until smooth. (For a note about how to deal with hot liquids in a blender, see page 16.) Refrigerate until cold, either in the blender canister or in a medium bowl, for at least 4 hours, or overnight.

4. Whisk or blend the mixture again, then freeze in your ice cream machine according to the manufacturer's instructions. Serve at once—or scoop into a large container, seal tightly, and store in the freezer for up to 1 month.

Classic Lemon Sherbet   Substitute ⅔ cup lemon juice, strained of all pulp, for the lime juice.

Tangerine Sherbet   Substitute ⅔ cup freshly squeezed tangerine juice for the lime juice.

Customize it!

Add any of the following to the blender with the lime juice: ¼ cup orange-flavored liqueur such as Cointreau, ¼ cup rum, ¼ cup tequila, ¼ cup vodka, 2 tablespoons chopped fresh mint leaves, or a few dashes of Tabasco sauce.

LYCHEE SHERBET

Makes about 1 quart (can be doubled for half-gallon machines)

Light, creamy, and full of perfume, lychee sherbet is best with a sugar cookie on the side—especially after Chinese take-out.

> 1 teaspoon unflavored gelatin
> 1 tablespoon cool water
> One 15-ounce can pitted lychees in syrup
> ⅓ cup light corn syrup
> ¼ teaspoon salt
> 2 cups whole milk

1. Sprinkle the gelatin over the water in a small bowl or a teacup; set aside to soften for 5 minutes.

2. Meanwhile, drain the lychees, reserving their syrup in a separate bowl. Place the lychees, corn syrup, and salt in a large blender; blend until smooth.

3. Warm the reserved lychee syrup in a small saucepan set over low heat. Reduce the heat to very low and stir in the gelatin mixture until dissolved, for no more than 20 seconds. Do not allow the mixture to come to a simmer. Set aside.

4. Pour the milk into the blender with the lychee puree; blend until smooth. Strain through a fine-mesh sieve into a medium bowl; stir in the syrup mixture until smooth. Refrigerate until cold, for at least 4 hours, or overnight.

5. Whisk the mixture again, then freeze in your ice cream machine according to the manufacturer's instructions. Serve at once—or scoop into a large container, seal well, and store in the freezer for up to 1 month.

Customize it!

Add any of the following to the blender with the lychee puree: 8 large hulled strawberries, ¼ cup ginger liqueur such as the Original Canton Ginger Liqueur, ¼ cup passion fruit concentrate (see Source Guide, page 241), 2 tablespoons ginger juice, 1 tablespoon grated lemon or lime zest.

MANGO SHERBET

Makes about 1 quart (can be doubled for half-gallon machines)

Use the freshest mangos you can find—they should smell like perfume even before you cut them open. Reserve all the precious juice when you chop the mango flesh, and add it to the blender as well.

> 2 large mangos, peeled, pitted, and chopped, juice reserved
> ¼ cup light corn syrup
> 1 tablespoon lime juice
> ¼ teaspoon salt
> 1¾ cups whole milk
> ½ cup sugar

1. Place the chopped mango and any juice in a blender; blend until fairly smooth, scraping down the sides of the canister as necessary. Add the corn syrup, lime juice, and salt; blend well and set aside.

2. Warm the milk in a medium saucepan over low heat. Stir in the sugar until dissolved. Pour this mixture into the blender with the mango puree. Blend until smooth. (For a note on how to deal with hot things in a blender, see page 16.) Strain through a fine-mesh sieve into a medium bowl and refrigerate until cold, for at least 4 hours, or overnight.

3. Freeze in your ice cream machine according to the manufacturer's instructions. Serve at once—or transfer to a large container, seal well, and store in the freezer for up to 1 month; soften at room temperature for 5 minutes before serving.

Customize it!
Add any of the following to the blender with the mango puree: 1 ripe peeled banana; ¼ cup coconut rum; ¼ cup frozen pineapple juice concentrate, thawed; ¼ cup frozen orange juice concentrate, thawed; ¼ cup honey; or 1 tablespoon vanilla extract.

Orange Sherbet

Makes about 1 quart (can be doubled for half-gallon machines)

Rather than using fresh orange juice in this tart sherbet, we recommend orange juice concentrate because it offers a flavor that's, well, more concentrated.

> **1 teaspoon unflavored gelatin**
> **1 tablespoon cool water**
> **2¼ cups whole milk**
> **½ cup sugar**
> **¼ cup light corn syrup**
> **¼ teaspoon salt**
> **One 12-ounce can frozen orange juice concentrate, thawed**

1. Sprinkle the gelatin over the water in a small bowl or teacup; set aside to soften for 5 minutes.

2. Warm 1¼ cups of the milk in a medium saucepan over low heat. Stir in the sugar and corn syrup until dissolved. Reduce the heat to very low and stir in the gelatin mixture and salt, just until dissolved, about 10 seconds. Do not allow the mixture to come to a simmer.

3. Transfer this warmed milk mixture to a large blender, add the orange juice concentrate and the remaining 1 cup milk, and blend until smooth. (For a note on how to treat hot liquids in a blender, see page 16.) Transfer to a bowl and refrigerate until cold, for about 4 hours, or overnight.

4. Whisk the mixture again, then freeze in your ice cream machine according to the manufacturer's instructions. Serve at once—or scoop into a large container and store in the freezer, sealed tightly, for up to 1 month.

Harvey Wallbanger Sherbet   Reduce the milk to 2 cups; warm 1 cup over low heat as directed. Add ¼ cup vodka and 2 tablespoons Galliano to the blender with the orange juice concentrate and the remaining milk.

Orange Julius Sherbet   Mix ¼ cup instant vanilla pudding mix into the blender with the orange juice concentrate.

Seabreeze Sherbet   Use a 6-ounce can of orange juice concentrate; add a 6-ounce can of frozen cranberry juice concentrate, thawed, to the blender with the remaining orange juice concentrate.

Screwdriver Sherbet   Add ¼ cup vodka to the blender with the orange juice concentrate.

Papaya Sherbet

Makes about 1 quart (can be doubled for half-gallon machines)

Have lots of sponge cake on hand to go with this tropical pleaser.

> **One 15-ounce can papaya chunks in syrup**
> **2 tablespoons lemon juice**
> **2 cups whole milk**
> **⅔ cup sugar**
> **¼ teaspoon salt**

1. Place the papaya and any syrup along with the lemon juice in a large blender; blend until smooth, scraping down the sides of the canister as necessary. Set aside.

2. Warm 1½ cups of the milk in a medium saucepan set over low heat. Stir in the sugar and salt until dissolved. Pour into the blender with the papaya puree, add the remaining ½ cup milk, and blend until smooth. (For a note on how to deal with hot liquids in a blender, see page 16.)

3. Strain the papaya mixture through a fine-mesh sieve into a medium bowl, gently pushing the solids against the mesh to extract all the liquid. Discard the solids, whisk well, and refrigerate until cold, for at least 4 hours, or overnight.

4. Whisk the mixture again, then freeze in your ice cream machine according to the manufacturer's instructions. Serve at once—or scoop into a large container, seal tightly, and store in the freezer for up to 1 month; soften at room temperature for 5 minutes before serving.

Customize it!
Reduce the milk to 1 cup; heat the entire amount as directed in step 2. Then add 1 cup of any of the following to the blender with the papaya puree: banana nectar, canned lychees with syrup, coconut milk, guanabana nectar, mango nectar, or peach nectar.

PASSION FRUIT SHERBET

Makes about 1 quart (can be doubled for half-gallon machines)

Passion fruit concentrate is a fine addition to any pantry; it's a little bit of sour extravagance that can be added to stir-fries or salad dressings—or a delicious sherbet. Look for the concentrate at Asian markets and from outlets listed in the Source Guide (page 241).

> 1 teaspoon unflavored gelatin
> 1 tablespoon cool water
> 2 cups whole milk
> ¾ cup sugar
> 1½ cups passion fruit concentrate

1. Sprinkle the gelatin over the water in a small bowl or a teacup; set aside to soften for 5 minutes.

2. Warm 1 cup of the milk in a medium saucepan set over low heat. Stir in the sugar until dissolved. Reduce the heat to very low and stir in the gelatin mixture until dissolved, for no more than 20 seconds. Do not allow the mixture to come to a simmer.

3. Pour into a large blender and add the remaining 1 cup milk and the passion fruit concentrate; blend until smooth. (For a note about dealing with hot things in a blender, see page 16.) Strain through a fine-mesh sieve into a medium bowl and refrigerate until well chilled, for at least 4 hours, or overnight.

4. Whisk the mixture again, then freeze in your ice cream machine according to the manufacturer's instructions. Serve at once—or scoop into a large container, seal well, and store in the freezer for up to 1 month.

Customize it!

Reduce the passion fruit concentrate to 1 cup and add ½ cup of any of the following frozen concentrate with the remaining passion fruit concentrate: cranberry juice concentrate, thawed; limeade concentrate, thawed; orange juice concentrate, thawed; pineapple juice concentrate, thawed; or raspberry juice concentrate, thawed.

PEACH SHERBET

Makes about 1 quart (can be doubled for half-gallon machines)

If the peaches you find are hard and odorless, place them in a paper bag, seal it loosely, and let it sit on your counter for up to 48 hours, until the peaches are soft and fragrant.

> **1 pound fresh peaches, peeled, pitted, and cut into wedges**
> **1 tablespoon lemon juice**
> **¼ teaspoon salt**
> **2½ cups whole milk**
> **⅔ cup sugar**

1. Place the peaches, lemon juice, and salt in a blender and blend until fairly smooth, scraping down the sides of the canister as necessary.

2. Warm 1½ cups of the milk in a medium saucepan set over low heat. Stir in the sugar until dissolved. Pour into the blender with the peach puree; add the remaining 1 cup milk. Blend until smooth. (For a note on how to deal with hot liquids in a blender, see page 16.) Strain through a fine-mesh sieve into a medium bowl and refrigerate until cold, for about 4 hours, or overnight.

3. Whisk the mixture again and freeze in your ice cream machine according to the manufacturer's instructions. Serve at once—or transfer to a large container, seal well, and store in the freezer for up to 1 month; soften at room temperature for 5 minutes before serving.

Nectarine Sherbet   Substitute ripe nectarines for the peaches.

Customize it!
Add any of the following to the blender with the peach or nectarine puree: 2 tablespoons white crème de cacao, 2 tablespoons white crème de

menthe, 2 tablespoons hazelnut syrup, 2 tablespoons Orgeat or almond syrup, 2 tablespoons peach schnapps, 2 tablespoons chopped fresh mint leaves, 2 tablespoons chopped fresh rosemary, 2 tablespoons chopped fresh thyme, 1 teaspoon maple flavoring, or 1 teaspoon rum extract.

PINEAPPLE SHERBET

Makes about 1 quart (can be doubled for half-gallon machines)

Among commercial brands, pineapple sherbet is the most popular in the U.S. No wonder—it's wonderfully sweet and sour, refreshing anytime.

> **One 20-ounce can pineapple chunks in syrup, drained**
> **1 tablespoon lime juice**
> **½ teaspoon vanilla extract**
> **2 cups whole milk**
> **¾ cup sugar**
> **¼ teaspoon salt**

1. Place the pineapple chunks, lime juice, and vanilla in a blender; blend until smooth, scraping down the sides of the canister as necessary. Set aside.

2. Warm the milk in a medium saucepan over low heat. Stir in the sugar and salt until dissolved. Cool for 10 minutes.

3. Pour the milk mixture into the blender with the pineapple puree. Blend until as smooth as possible. (For a note about how to treat hot liquids in a blender, see page 16.) Strain through a fine-mesh sieve into a medium bowl, pressing against the solids with the back of a wooden spoon to release as much liquid as possible. Discard the solids and refrigerate the mixture until cold, for at least 4 hours, or overnight.

4. Whisk the mixture, then freeze in your ice cream machine according to the manufacturer's instructions. Serve at once—or scoop into a large container, seal tightly, and store in the freezer for up to 1 month; soften at room temperature for 5 minutes before serving.

Piña Colada Sherbet   Substitute 2 cups coconut milk for the milk.

Customize it!

Add any of the following to the blender with the pineapple puree: 1 ripe peeled banana; 1 fresh seeded and stemmed jalapeño chile pepper; ¼ cup frozen orange juice concentrate, thawed; ¼ cup vanilla-flavored liqueur such as Licor 43; 2 tablespoons chopped fresh basil; 2 tablespoons chopped fresh mint leaves; or 1 tablespoon chopped fresh thyme.

RASPBERRY SHERBET

Makes about 1 quart (can be doubled for half-gallon machines)

While raspberries are best in summer's heat, you can use frozen raspberries for this simple, creamy sherbet.

> 1½ cups (¾ pint) fresh raspberries, or 12 ounces frozen raspberries, thawed, all juice reserved
> 1 tablespoon lemon juice
> ¼ teaspoon salt
> 1¾ cups whole milk
> ½ cup sugar
> ¼ cup light corn syrup

1. Place the raspberries, lemon juice, and salt in a large blender; blend until smooth, scraping down the sides of the canister as necessary. Set aside.

2. Warm 1 cup of the milk in a medium saucepan over low heat. Stir in the sugar and corn syrup until dissolved. Pour into the blender with the raspberry puree, add the remaining ¾ cup milk, and blend until fairly smooth. (For a note on how to deal with hot things in a blender, see page 16.) Strain through a fine-mesh sieve into a medium bowl, gently pressing the mass against the mesh with the back of a wooden spoon to extract as much of the liquid as possible while leaving the seeds behind. Refrigerate until cold, for about 4 hours, or overnight.

3. Whisk the mixture, then freeze in your ice cream machine according to the manufacturer's instructions. Serve at once—or transfer to a large container, seal tightly, and store in the freezer for up to 1 month; soften at room temperature for 5 minutes before serving.

Blackberry Sherbet Substitute blackberries for the raspberries. Decrease the lemon juice to 1 teaspoon.

White Raspberry Sherbet   Substitute white raspberries for the regular raspberries.

Customize it!
Add 2 tablespoons chopped fresh mint leaves to the blender with the raspberry puree.

Or substitute 2 teaspoons grated orange zest for the lemon juice.

STRAWBERRY SHERBET

Makes about 1 quart (can be doubled for half-gallon machines)

Have lots of cookies on hand to go with this summery sherbet—or serve it along-side the Chocolate Granita (page 140).

>   3 cups (1½ pints) fresh strawberries, hulled
>   1 tablespoon lemon or lime juice
>   ¼ teaspoon salt
>   1¾ cups whole milk
>   ⅔ cup sugar

1. Place the strawberries, lemon or lime juice, and salt in a large blender; blend until smooth, scraping down the sides of the canister as necessary. Set aside.

2. Warm 1 cup of the milk in a medium saucepan over low heat. Stir in the sugar until dissolved. Pour into the blender with the strawberry puree, add the remaining ¾ cup milk, and blend until fairly smooth. (For a note on how to deal with hot things in a blender, see page 16.) Strain through a fine-mesh sieve into a medium bowl, gently pressing the mass against the mesh with the back of a wooden spoon to extract as much of the liquid as possible while leaving the seeds behind. Refrigerate until cold, for about 4 hours, or overnight.

3. Whisk the mixture, then freeze in your ice cream machine according to the manufacturer's instructions. Serve at once—or transfer to a large container, seal tightly, and store in your freezer for up to 1 month; soften at room temperature for 5 minutes before serving.

Customize it!
Add any of the following to the blender with the strawberry puree: ¼ cup no-bake cheesecake powder, 2 tablespoons chopped fresh mint leaves, 2 tablespoons chopped fresh tarragon leaves, 2 tablespoons chopped fresh thyme, 1 tablespoon grated orange zest, 1 tablespoon vanilla extract, 1 teaspoon almond extract, 1 teaspoon freshly ground black pepper, or 1 teaspoon banana extract.

Granita

A granita is the simplest of all frozen desserts: just fruit and sugar, cooked or sometimes just blended, poured into a 9 × 13-inch baking pan, placed in the freezer, and stirred with a fork a few times while it chills. A couple of hours later, you a have a pan of jewel-like ice crystals which you scrape up and mound in a dessert cup or even a martini glass. Cold, crunchy, sweet, and refreshing—what could be better? Oh, fat free, too.

All that stirring and scraping are designed to break up the ice crystals as they freeze, preventing the concoction from becoming a solid block. In fact, granite (gra-nee-TAY, the plural of *granita*) are so named in Italian because they look like clear, sandy grains in a glass.

If you want to start easy, just testing out the technique, pour two cans of carbonated soda in a 9 × 13-inch baking pan, place it on the floor of the freezer, and freeze for about 2 hours, stirring every 20 minutes or so to get the ice crystals broken up and even. Scrape up with a fork and enjoy.

Granite are related to "water ices" in that they too are icy pleasures without cream or eggs. But those are creamier than granite, often made with corn syrup, sometimes even churned in an ice cream machine. A granita is more like shaved ice, sometimes called "Italian ice," a treat popular on the streets of New York City in the August blaze. Vendors push around little carts from which they scrape the icy mixture into little cups; you slurp it up without a spoon.

But the real thing is grainier still, the result of a little patience and even less effort—no more than a few stirrings over a couple of hours.

SUPERFINE SUGAR

Many of these recipes call for no cooking at all—just blend and freeze. In these, we call for superfine sugar, a favorite of bartenders. It's granulated sugar ground to a fine powder so it will dissolve quickly. Look for superfine sugar in the baking or the drinks aisle of your supermarket.

WANT TO SKIP ALL THAT STIRRING?

Pour any of the following mixtures into two or three ice-cube trays and freeze without stirring, for at least 3 hours. (Trays vary in size, so there's no way to say exactly how many you'll need.) Unmold the cubes into a large food processor fitted with the chopping blade and pulse a few times until icy. It's not exactly the same consistency—the crystals are a little more watery—but it's certainly a no-hassle approach to this Italian favorite.

THREE TIPS FOR GRANITA SUCCESS

1. Place the baking pan right on the floor of your freezer, the coldest part. When you stir up the granita for the last time, smooth it out so that the surface is level, without little bunches of crystals that harden into lumps. After the last stirring, cover the pan with plastic wrap to protect the granita from freezer odors.

2. Self-defrosting freezers can murder a good granita; the constant change in temperature will ruin those sparkly crystals you've worked to create. If you have a self-defrosting freezer, it's best to eat the granita within a day of making it.

3. A fancy, stemmed glass—such as a wineglass, a martini glass, or a brandy snifter—works best to show off a granita when you serve it.

APPLE GRANITA

Makes about 4 cups of shaved ice

Don't think of this tart granita as only a summer pleasure. Why not try it after a stew in the fall? Or serve it between courses at your next blowout affair.

> 1¼ cups unsweetened apple juice
> 1 cup sugar
> 2 pounds Granny Smith apples, cored and chopped
> 1 tablespoon lemon juice
> ⅛ teaspoon salt

1. Bring the juice and sugar to a simmer in a large saucepan over high heat, stirring just until the sugar dissolves. Add the apples, lemon juice, and salt. Cover the pan, reduce the heat, and simmer for 10 minutes. Set aside to cool at room temperature for 20 minutes.

2. Pour the apple mixture into a large blender or a food processor fitted with the chopping blade. Blend or process until pureed, then strain through a fine-mesh sieve into a 9 × 13-inch baking pan, gently pressing against the solids with the back of a wooden spoon to remove as much juice as possible. Discard the solids.

3. Freeze on the floor of the freezer for about 3 hours, stirring with a fork about every 20 minutes to break up the ice crystals and allow more of the liquid to come into contact with the pan. Once the granita is frozen but still soft, smooth out the crystals and cover the pan with plastic wrap. Tightly covered, the granita can be stored in the freezer for up to 3 weeks.

4. Scrape up the ice crystals from the granita's surface with a fork. Mound these into cups, bowls, or glasses; serve at once.

Apple Ginger Granita   Add one 4-inch piece of fresh ginger, peeled and cut into rings, to the saucepan with the apples. Discard before blending.

Apple Lemongrass Granita　Add 1 lemongrass stalk, chopped into 1-inch segments and crushed with the side of a knife, to the saucepan with the apples. Discard before blending.

Pear Granita　Substitute 2 pounds ripe pears, cored and chopped, for the apples.

Customize it!

Add any of the following to the saucepan before you set it aside to cool for 20 minutes: 1 orange cut into six sections, 1 lemon cut into quarters, ¼ cup brandy, ¼ cup Calvados, 2 teaspoons chopped fresh thyme, 2 teaspoons chopped fresh mint leaves, or 1 teaspoon chopped tarragon.

CHAMPAGNE GRANITA

Makes about 4 cups of shaved ice

There may be no more elegant granita, sweet and tart. It's a fine finish to any meal, especially alongside some fresh macaroons.

> **2 cups Champagne, Prosecco, or sparkling wine**
> **1 cup unsweetened apple juice or white grape juice**
> **½ cup sugar, preferably superfine**

1. Whisk all ingredients together in a bowl until the sugar dissolves and the foaming just starts to subside (some foaming will help the granita stay light and airy as it freezes). Pour into a 9 x 13-inch baking pan. Freeze on the floor of the freezer for about 2 hours, stirring with a fork every 20 minutes. When the granita is frozen but soft, smooth out the crystals and cover the pan with plastic wrap. Tightly sealed, the granita can stay in the freezer for up to 2 weeks.

2. Serve by scraping up the ice crystals with a fork and mounding them in cups, bowls, or glasses.

Wine Granita Substitute red or white wine for the champagne; increase the sugar to ¾ cup.

Sweet Dessert Wine Granita Omit the apple juice and use 3 cups vin santo sweet Marsala or port; decrease the sugar to ¼ cup.

CHERRY GRANITA

Makes about 3 cups of shaved ice

Sour cherries work best in this perky indulgence. Fresh, they have a short shelf-life; so use jarred cherries for a year-round treat. Check to make sure they're whole and firm in the jar.

> **One 24-ounce jar pitted sour cherries**
> **½ cup sugar, preferably superfine sugar**
> **1 tablespoon lemon juice**
> **⅛ teaspoon salt**

1. Place the sour cherries and all the liquid from the jar along with the sugar, lemon juice, and salt in a large blender. Blend until as smooth as possible. (You can work in batches, if necessary.) Strain through a fine-mesh sieve into a 9 × 13-inch baking pan, gently pushing against the solids with the back of a wooden spoon to remove as much juice as possible. Discard the solids.

2. Freeze on the floor of the freezer for about 2 hours, stirring it with a fork about every 20 minutes to break the ice crystals apart and spread them throughout the mixture. After the mixture has frozen but is still soft, even out the ice crystals and cover the pan tightly with plastic wrap. The granita can be stored in the freezer, tightly covered, for up to 3 weeks.

3. Serve by scraping the surface of the granita with a fork to render as many ice crystals as possible; scoop these into individual-serving glasses, cups, or bowls.

Customize it!
Add any of the following to the blender with the cherries: ¼ cup Armagnac, ¼ cup brandy, 2 teaspoons vanilla extract, 1 teaspoon almond extract, 1 teaspoon rum extract, or ½ teaspoon mint extract.

CHOCOLATE GRANITA

Makes a little less than 4 cups of shaved ice

Here's the one granita that's not made from fruit. It's an Italian classic—a dense, dark chocolate mixture that stirs up into grains of Paradise.

> 2 cups water
> 1 cup sugar
> 1 cup cocoa powder, sifted
> 1 teaspoon vanilla extract
> ⅛ teaspoon salt

1. Whisk the water and sugar in a heavy saucepan set over medium-high heat until the sugar dissolves. Whisk in the cocoa powder, vanilla, and salt until smooth; bring to a simmer. Reduce the heat and simmer for 2 minutes. Remove from the heat and cool at room temperature for 15 minutes.

2. Stir well and pour the mixture into a 9 × 13-inch baking pan; place it on the floor of the freezer. Freeze for about 2 hours, stirring about every 20 minutes with a fork to get the ice crystals off the bottom and away from the sides of the pan. When they're frozen but still soft, smooth out the crystals and cover the pan with plastic wrap. The granita can be kept this way in the freezer for up to 2 weeks.

3. To serve, scrape with a fork, creating lots of icy shards; mound into cups or glasses.

Customize it!
Stir any of the following into the pan after the mixture has cooled: 2 teaspoons orange extract, 1 teaspoon almond extract, 1 teaspoon rum extract, or ½ teaspoon mint extract.

COFFEE GRANITA

Makes a little less than 4 cups of shaved ice

If you don't have an espresso maker, use instant espresso powder to make the coffee for this sophisticated granita. Use 7 teaspoons of powder for 2½ cups of water.

> 2½ cups brewed espresso
> ¼ cup coffee-flavored liqueur, such as Kahlúa
> ⅔ cup sugar, preferably superfine sugar
> 1 teaspoon grated lemon zest, finely chopped

1. Whisk all the ingredients in a large bowl until the sugar dissolves, pour into a 9 × 13-inch baking pan; place it on the floor of the freezer. Freeze for about 2 hours, scraping and stirring with a fork every 20 minutes or so to break apart the ice crystals and distribute them throughout the mixture. When the granita is frozen but still soft, smooth out the crystals and cover the pan with plastic wrap. The granita can be stored, tightly covered, in the freezer for up to 3 weeks.

2. Serve by scraping up the ice crystals from the granita's surface with a fork; scoop them into individual-serving bowls, plates, or cups.

You can endlessly vary this recipe based on the coffee you use, anything from different roasts to flavored beans.

Sicily is known for a heavenly dessert made with coffee granita. Beat 2 cups of heavy cream until doubled in volume, then stir the scraped-up ice crystals into the whipped cream and serve at once.

Concord Grape Granita

Makes about 3 cups of shaved ice

Think of this granita as a frozen version of grape jelly. A rare treat would be to sprinkle these icy granules over Peanut Butter Gelato (page 75). Concord grapes show up in our markets in late summer and early fall.

> **1 pound Concord grapes, stems removed**
> **1½ cups unsweetened white grape juice**
> **½ cup sugar**
> **⅛ teaspoon salt**

1. Bring the grapes, grape juice, sugar, and salt to a boil in a large saucepan set over high heat. Cover, reduce the heat, and simmer slowly until the grapes soften and pop open, about 2 minutes. Steep off the heat, covered, for 45 minutes.

2. Place the mixture in a large sieve set over a large bowl (you may work in batches, if necessary). Press the mixture through the sieve with the back of a wooden spoon, thereby straining out the skins and seeds. (Alternatively, you can put the mixture through a food mill.) Pour the strained mixture into a 9 x 13-inch baking pan; discard the solids.

3. Freeze the mixture in the pan on the floor of the freezer for about 2 hours, stirring about every 20 minutes with a fork to redistribute the ice crystals in the granita. When it's frozen but still soft, smooth out the crystals and cover the pan with plastic wrap. Tightly covered, the granita can be stored in the freezer for up to 3 weeks.

4. To serve, scrape up the ice crystals from the granita's surface with a fork and mound them in cups, glasses, or bowls.

Customize it!

Add any of the following to the saucepan before you set it aside to steep, but remove them before you blend the mixture in the pan: two 4-inch cinnamon sticks; two large strips of lemon zest; two large strips of orange zest; one 4-inch piece of fresh ginger, peeled and cut into rings; or 1 lemongrass stalk, cut into 1-inch segments and bruised with the side of a knife.

CRANBERRY GRANITA

Makes about 4 cups of shaved ice

If you're making this refresher anytime other than the late fall, you'll probably have to use frozen cranberries. Don't defrost them—just add them straight to the saucepan.

    2½ **cups water**
    2 **cups whole cranberries (about 8 ounces)**
    1 **cup sugar**
    ⅛ **teaspoon salt**

1. Place all the ingredients in a large saucepan and bring to a simmer over medium-high heat, stirring just until the sugar dissolves. Reduce the heat and simmer until the berries have softened, about 10 minutes. Cover and cool off the heat for 20 minutes.

2. Pour the contents of the pan into a large blender and puree until smooth. Strain through a fine-mesh sieve into a 9 × 13-inch baking pan, pushing the solids against the mesh with the back of a wooden spoon.

3. Freeze the mixture in the pan on the floor of the freezer for about 3 hours, stirring about every 20 minutes with a fork to break up the ice crystals and distribute them evenly throughout the pan. After the mixture has frozen but is not yet fully firm, cover it tightly with plastic wrap. The granita will keep this way for up to 3 weeks.

4. Scrape the surface of the granita with a fork to produce lots of shaved ice crystals; scoop these into individual cups or glasses for serving.

Spiced Cranberry Granita   Add 1 teaspoon ground cinnamon, ¼ teaspoon ground mace, and ¼ teaspoon grated nutmeg to the pan before you set the mixture aside to cool for 20 minutes.

GRAPEFRUIT GRANITA

Makes about 4 cups of shaved ice

Bottled grapefruit juice is sometimes sweetened—and the heating process necessary to preserving the juice often mutes its taste. For the best results, use only fresh grapefruit juice.

¾ **cup water**
½ **cup sugar**
2¼ **cups freshly squeezed grapefruit juice (from about 2 large grapefruits)**
⅛ **teaspoon salt**

1. Bring the water and sugar to a boil in a large saucepan set over high heat, stirring just until the sugar dissolves. The moment the mixture boils, remove it from the heat and cool at room temperature for 10 minutes.

2. Stir in the grapefruit juice and salt. Pour into a 9 × 13-inch baking pan and freeze on the floor of the freezer for about 3 hours, stirring with a fork every 20 minutes or so to distribute the ice crystals evenly throughout the mixture. After the mixture has frozen fully but is still soft, flatten it out in the pan and cover with plastic wrap. Tightly wrapped, the granita can be stored in the freezer for up to 2 weeks.

3. To serve, scrape up the ice crystals from the granita's surface with a fork; gather these together and scoop them into individual-serving bowls, cups, or glasses.

Customize it!
Stir any of the following into the mixture with the grapefruit juice: ¼ cup Blue Curaçao, ¼ cup Campari, ¼ cup Galliano, 2 teaspoons chopped fresh thyme, 2 teaspoons chopped fresh mint leaves, 1 teaspoon chopped fresh rosemary, or 1 teaspoon chopped fresh tarragon.

KIWI GRANITA

Makes about 4 cups of shaved ice

The condensed sweetness of a cooked sugar syrup quickly overpowers kiwis, so here's the simplest granita of all—no cooking; just blend, strain, and freeze.

> 6 large kiwi fruit, peeled and halved
> 1½ cups sugar, preferably superfine sugar
> 1½ cups water
> 1 tablespoon lemon juice
> ⅛ teaspoon salt

1. Place all the ingredients in a large blender or a food processor fitted with the chopping blade. Puree until as smooth as possible. Strain through a fine-mesh sieve into a 9 × 13-inch baking pan to remove the seeds and any pulpy bits.

2. Freeze on the floor of the freezer for about 2 hours, stirring with a fork about every 20 minutes to break apart the ice crystals. When the mixture is frozen but soft, even out the granita and cover the pan with plastic wrap. The granita will keep, tightly covered, in the freezer for up to 2 weeks.

3. Serve by scraping up the ice crystals with a fork from the granita's surface; scoop them into individual serving glasses or bowls.

Kiwi Cocktail Granita Add ¼ cup white rum or vodka with the ingredients in the blender.

LEMON GRANITA

Makes about 4 cups of shaved ice

For a real hit at your next get-together, serve this summery treat with sugar cookies—or even in sugar ice cream cones.

> 1¼ **cups sugar**
> 1¼ **cups water**
> 1¼ **cups lemon juice (from about 8 medium lemons)**
> ⅛ **teaspoon salt**

1. Mix the sugar and water in a medium saucepan set over medium-high heat until the sugar dissolves. Bring the mixture to a simmer, reduce the heat, and simmer for 3 minutes. Cool at room temperature for 10 minutes in the pan. Stir in the lemon juice and salt.

2. Pour this mixture into a 9 × 13-inch baking pan and place on the floor of the freezer. Freeze for about 2 hours, stirring with a fork about every 20 minutes, until icy but smooth, with distinct ice crystals. Smooth out the granita and cover the pan tightly with plastic wrap. The granita can be stored this way in your freezer for up to 3 weeks.

3. To serve, scrape the surface of the granita with a fork, rendering lots of small crystals; scoop them into cups or glasses.

Customize it!
Stir in any of the following with the lemon juice: ¼ cup gin, ¼ cup gold rum, ¼ cup raspberry-flavored liqueur such as Chambord, ¼ cup tequila, 1 tablespoon chopped fresh mint leaves, 1 tablespoon chopped fresh thyme, or 2 teaspoons chopped fresh tarragon leaves.

LIME GRANITA

Makes about 4 cups of shaved ice

For a creamy treat, top this tart refresher with plain yogurt.

> 1⅓ cups sugar
> 1 cup water
> 1 tablespoon grated lime zest (from about 2 limes)
> 1⅓ cups lime juice (from about 12 medium limes)
> ⅛ teaspoon salt

1. Bring the water, sugar, and lime zest to a boil in a large saucepan, stirring just until the sugar dissolves. The moment the mixture boils, remove the pan from the heat and cool at room temperature for 10 minutes. Stir in the lime juice and salt.

2. Strain through a fine-mesh sieve into a 9 × 13-inch baking pan and freeze on the floor of the freezer for about 3 hours, stirring every 20 minutes or so with a fork to break up the ice crystals, particularly those that form along the bottom and sides of the pan and in the corners. When the mixture has frozen fully but is still soft, smooth it out in the pan and cover with plastic wrap. Tightly covered, the granita can be stored in the freezer for up to 2 weeks.

3. Serve by scraping the surface of the granita with a fork to break up the ice crystals; scoop them into individual-serving bowls or glasses.

Cosmopolitan Granita   Reduce the water to ¾ cup and the lime juice to 1 cup. Stir in ⅓ cup frozen cranberry juice concentrate, thawed, and ¼ cup vodka with the remaining lime juice.

Daiquiri Granita   Reduce the water to ¾ cup; stir in ¼ cup white rum with the lime juice.

Margarita Granita   Reduce the water to ¾ cup and the lime juice to 1 cup. Stir in ⅓ cup frozen orange juice concentrate, thawed, and ¼ cup tequila with the remaining lime juice.

Metropolitan Granita   Reduce the water to ¾ cup and the lime juice to 1 cup. Stir in ⅓ cup frozen cranberry juice concentrate, thawed, and ¼ cup currant-flavored vodka with the remaining lime juice.

ORANGE GRANITA

Makes about 5 cups of shaved ice

What could be better after a large meal than this cool palate-cleanser? It's enough to make even the deepest winter day seem like a stroll on the beach.

¾ **cup sugar**
¾ **cup water**
1 **tablespoon grated orange zest**
2¼ **cups freshly squeezed orange juice (from about 10 large oranges, maybe more)**
⅛ **teaspoon salt**

1. Bring the sugar, water, and orange zest to a boil in a large saucepan set over high heat, stirring just until the sugar dissolves. Reduce the heat and simmer for 1 minute. Cool at room temperature off the heat for 10 minutes, then stir in the orange juice and salt.

2. Strain through a fine-mesh sieve into a 9 × 13-inch baking dish and freeze on the floor of the freezer for about 3 hours, stirring with a fork about every 20 minutes to break up the ice crystals and distribute them evenly throughout the granita. When it's fully frozen but still soft, smooth out the crystals without pressing down and cover the pan with plastic wrap. Tightly covered, the granita can be stored in the freezer for up to 3 weeks.

3. To serve, scrape up the ice crystals from the granita's surface with a fork and scoop these into bowls, glasses, or cups.

Customize it!
Add any of the following with the orange juice: ¼ cup Campari, 2 teaspoons chopped fresh mint leaves, 2 teaspoons chopped fresh thyme, or 1 teaspoon chopped fresh rosemary.

PASSION FRUIT GRANITA

Makes about 4 cups of shaved ice

The passion fruit is a tropical jewel: sugary but tart. Rather than pitting the wrinkled fruits for hours, we recommend using passion fruit concentrate, available from many gourmet markets, most Asian markets, and outlets listed in the Source Guide (page 241).

> 2¼ cups water
> 1⅓ cups sugar
> 1 cup passion fruit concentrate
> 1 tablespoon lemon juice
> ⅛ teaspoon salt

1. Bring the water and sugar to a boil in a large saucepan set over high heat, stirring just until the sugar dissolves. Reduce the heat and simmer for 1 minute. Cool at room temperature for 10 minutes, then stir in the passion fruit concentrate, lemon juice, and salt.

2. Pour this mixture into a 9 × 13-inch baking pan and freeze on the floor of the freezer for about 3 hours, scraping the mixture with a fork about every 20 minutes to break up the ice crystals, particularly along the pan's bottom and sides and in the corners. Once the mixture is frozen but still soft, even out the ice crystals and cover the pan with plastic wrap. Tightly wrapped, the granita can be stored in the freezer for up to 2 weeks.

3. Scrape up the ice crystals from the granita's surface with a fork; scoop them into individual bowls or cups to serve.

Customize it!
Reduce the water to 1¾ cups and add ½ cup of any of these: banana nectar; mango juice; frozen orange juice concentrate, thawed; or frozen pineapple juice concentrate, thawed.

Raspberry Granita

Makes about 4 cups of shaved ice

While fresh raspberries definitely offer the best flavor in this icy treat, you can substitute frozen berries; soften them for about 20 minutes at room temperature before adding them to the blender.

> **1¼ cups water**
> **⅔ cup sugar**
> **1½ cups fresh raspberries (about 12 ounces), or 12 ounces frozen raspberries, thawed, along with all liquid in the package**
> **2 tablespoons lemon juice**
> **⅛ teaspoon salt**

1. Bring the water and sugar to a boil in a medium saucepan set over high heat, stirring just until the sugar dissolves. Cool at room temperature for 5 minutes.

2. Pour the sugar syrup into a large blender and add the raspberries, lemon juice, and salt. Blend until smooth. Strain through a fine-mesh sieve into a 9 × 13-inch baking pan, removing the seeds and the pulpy mass from the berries; gently press this mass against the mesh with the back of a wooden spoon to extract as much juice as you can.

3. Freeze on the floor of the freezer for about 3 hours, stirring with a fork about every 20 minutes to break up the ice crystals and distribute them throughout the mixture. After the granita has frozen but is still soft, cover the pan with plastic wrap. The granita can be kept this way in the freezer for up to 3 weeks.

4. Scrape the surface of the granita with a fork, thereby loosening lots of ice crystals from the mass. Scoop these into individual cups or glasses and serve at once.

Customize it!

Add any of the following to the blender with the raspberries: ¼ cup almond-flavored liqueur such as Amaretto, ¼ cup chocolate-flavored liqueur such as Godiva, ¼ cup raspberry-flavored liqueur such as Chambord, ¼ cup white rum, ¼ cup vodka, or 1 tablespoon chopped fresh mint leaves.

STRAWBERRY GRANITA

Makes about 4 cups of shaved ice

Here's a way to capture the summery freshness of strawberries in a simple granita. Great on its own, the little crystals are also terrific atop Blueberry Sherbet (page 109).

> 1 quart strawberries, hulled and sliced
> 2 cups water
> ¾ cup plus 2 tablespoons sugar, preferably superfine sugar
> 3 tablespoons lemon juice
> ¼ teaspoon salt

1. Place all the ingredients in a large food processor fitted with the chopping blade or in a large blender (work in batches in the blender if you need to). Process or blend until smooth.

2. Pour the mixture into a fine-mesh strainer set over a large bowl; set aside until the dripping stops, about 25 minutes. You can occasionally gather the mixture together to get it dripping more quickly, but do not press the applesauce-thick solids against the mesh so the juice remains as clear as possible.

3. Pour the strained juice into a 9 × 13-inch baking pan and freeze on your freezer's floor for about 2 hours, stirring with a fork every 20 minutes or so to break up the ice crystals. Once the mixture is frozen, smooth it out and cover the pan with plastic wrap. The granita can be stored this way for up to 2 weeks.

4. To serve, scrape up the crystals with a fork, mounding them into a glass or cup.

Customize it!
Add any of the following to the food processor or blender with the other ingredients: ¼ cup white rum, 3 tablespoons chopped fresh mint leaves, 2 tablespoons balsamic vinegar, 2 tablespoons chopped fresh tarragon leaves, 1 tablespoon freshly ground black pepper, 1 teaspoon almond extract, 1 teaspoon banana extract, 1 teaspoon rum extract, or a few dashes of Tabasco sauce.

Tea Granita

Makes about 4 cups of shaved ice

Like frozen iced tea, this thirst-quencher needs only a sprig of mint to make it the perfect summer pleasure.

> 3 cups water
> 8 bags black tea, or 4 tablespoons loose black tea
> ⅔ cup sugar, preferably superfine sugar

1. Bring the water to a boil in a large saucepan set over high heat; remove from the heat and add the tea bags or stir in the loose tea. Cover and set aside to steep at room temperature for up to 30 minutes.

2. Remove the tea bags; if using loose tea, strain the mixture to get rid of the leaves. Stir in the sugar until dissolved, then pour into a 9 × 13-inch baking pan. Freeze on the floor of the freezer for about 2 hours, stirring with a fork to break up the ice crystals. When the granita is fully frozen but still soft, smooth out the crystals and cover the pan with plastic wrap. Tightly covered, the granita can be stored in the freezer for up to 3 weeks.

3. Serve by scraping up the ice crystals with a fork and mounding them in individual-serving cups, bowls, or glasses.

Lemon Tea Granita   Stir in the juice of half a lemon with the sugar.

Customize it!
Use any flavor of tea you want, from Earl Grey to herbal—or use a decaf tea.

WATERMELON GRANITA

Makes about 4 cups of shaved ice

Shave this candy-red granita into martini glasses and top each with a shot of chilled lemon vodka.

> **6 cups red or yellow watermelon cubes, preferably seedless watermelon— if not, then seeds removed**
> **⅓ cup sugar, preferably superfine sugar**
> **1 tablespoon lime juice**
> **1 tablespoon grenadine (see Note)**
> **⅛ teaspoon salt**

1. Place all the ingredients in a large blender or a food processor fitted with the chopping blade. Blend or pulse until fairly smooth. (You can work in batches, if necessary.) Strain through a fine-mesh sieve into a 9 × 13-inch baking dish to remove any stringy solids and place on the floor of the freezer. Freeze for about 3 hours, stirring with a fork about every 20 minutes, until icy but smooth, with distinct ice crystals. Even out the crystals and cover the pan tightly with plastic wrap. The granita can be kept this way in the freezer for up to 2 weeks.

2. To serve, scrape the surface of the granita with a fork, rendering lots of small crystals; scoop them into cups or glasses.

NOTE: Grenadine, once exclusively made on the Caribbean island of Grenada, is a sweet red syrup flavored with pomegranate. Some bottlings include alcohol; it's best to use one without the buzz for this recipe.

Spicy Watermelon Granita   Spike it up by adding a few dashes of Tabasco sauce to the blender with the other ingredients.

Semifreddo

Although the Italian name may say otherwise, there's nothing "half frozen" about a semifreddo. It's *all* frozen—there's just too much sugar, egg white, and whipped cream for it to freeze solid. It's more like a "semi-gelato": some halfway point between a frozen custard and a frozen mousse, put into a loaf pan, frozen, sliced, and served on plates, to be eaten with a fork, not a spoon.

Traditionally, semifreddi (the plural in Italian) are served as midafternoon perk-ups. It's a modern invention, a kind of Italian cold shoulder to French pastries. As in most Italian treats, the emphasis is not on a complicated pastry cream but on straightforward tastes, although here fussed up about as much as any Italian dessert can be.

There's a great divide among semifreddo mavens over the texture of this frozen treat. Some prefer a creamy consistency, sort of like an ice cream terrine in a loaf pan. In fact, some restaurants serve ice cream in slices, calling it semifreddi. Good and satisfying, but hardly the real thing.

We're unabashed in our preference for soft, marshmallowy, luxurious semifreddi. Admittedly, achieving these results takes a little work. First, you whip up a modified zabaglione: a mixture of egg yolks and sugar, sometimes with a liquor, beaten over a pot of simmering water. Then you make a version of seven-minute frosting: egg whites and sugar, again beaten over simmering water. Finally, you combine both with whipped cream. Spoon it into a loaf pan and try to wait for it to chill.

If you want to sample before you commit, we suggest the Easy Semifreddo (page 163). Purists, look elsewhere—but this no-cook concoction of Marshmallow Fluff, heavy cream, and sugar freezes up in a way that's incredibly similar to the real thing. We hope it's enough to convince you to make the real thing.

CUSTOMIZING THE SEMIFREDDI

Because the soft texture of semifreddi is so important, they can be customized with only a relatively small range of mix-ins. Use a standard 9 × 5-inch loaf pan; fold ¾ cup of any of the following or any combination of the following into the whipped cream before folding it into the semifreddo mixture: butterscotch chips, chopped hazelnuts, chopped pecans, chopped walnuts, Heath Bits, M&M's Mini Baking Bits, mini chocolate chips, peanut butter chips, Reese's Pieces, semisweet chocolate chips, shaved bittersweet chocolate, sliced almonds, sweetened shredded coconut, or white chocolate chips.

The tastes of any of the nuts or the coconut can be deepened by toasting—it's a matter of personal preference. To toast the nuts or the coconut, bake them on a large baking sheet in a preheated 350°F oven until fragrant, stirring frequently, for 4 to 8 minutes.

You can also vary the flavor of the Chocolate Semifreddo (page 161), the Nougat Semifreddo (page 170), the Nutty Semifreddo (page 172), the Ricotta Semifreddo (page 174), or the Vanilla Semifreddo (page 176) by beating ¼ cup of any of the following into the egg yolks before you beat them with the sugar over the simmering water: almond-flavored liqueur such as Amaretto, banana-flavored liqueur such as crème de banane, cherry-flavored liqueur such as Cherry Heering, chocolate-flavored liqueur such as Godiva, coffee-flavored liqueur such as Kahlúa, hazelnut-flavored liqueur such as Frangelico, or orange-flavored liqueur such as Cointreau.

Ten Tips to Semifreddo Success

1. We suggest using a 1-quart loaf pan (4 × 9 × 2¼ inches), slightly smaller than the standard 5 × 9-inch loaf pan. The semifreddo mounds a little higher, so you can slice off "taller" pieces that look better on a plate. Of course, you can use a standard loaf pan—no change in taste, just aesthetics.

2. Line the pan with plastic wrap but leave quite a bit hanging over the sides. The excess will allow you to pull the semifreddo out of the pan more easily once it's set. And place the lined pan in the freezer while you make the components of the semifreddo. A cold pan will help the dessert freeze evenly and quickly.

3. For the best height in beaten cream, make sure it's cold, just out of the refrigerator. It also helps if the bowl and the mixer's beaters are cold. For exceptionally dense whipped cream, beat the cream in a food processor fitted with the chopping blade.

4. Don't use a double boiler for either the egg-yolk or the egg-white mixtures. Although both must be beaten over simmering water, use heat-safe bowls that fit snugly over a saucepan. Watch out for the cord from your mixer—don't let it get in the water or near the heating element. You can use a whisk, but you'll need Popeye forearms.

5. Have all the ingredients prepped in advance. It's a three-bowl technique: one bowl for the whipped cream, one for the egg yolks and their additives, and one for the egg whites. And make the components in that order: 1) whipped cream, 2) zabaglione, and 3) seven-minute frosting.

6. The egg-yolk mixture should be beaten until it "mounds"—in other words, until it's thick enough to hold its shape. Turn off the beaters and lift them out of the pale yellow mixture; the small amounts that dribble off the beaters should not sink back in but should stay visible on top.

7. Freeze the semifreddo in the coldest part of the freezer—usually the floor, particularly the floor adjacent to the back wall. Because the mixture will not freeze hard, it's sometimes difficult to tell when it's ready—plan on 8 hours, maybe 6 hours if your freezer is exceptionally efficient.

8. To unmold a semifreddo, turn it upside down on a serving platter and wipe the bottom and sides of the loaf pan with a wad of paper towels that have been soaked in hot water and then wrung dry. They should be hot enough to loosen the sides of the pan slightly without any fear of drenching the dessert in water.

9. Use a serrated knife to cut a semifreddo. Don't dip the knife in warm water—that will only waterlog the dessert.

10. If you haven't sliced up the whole loaf, cover the remainder with plastic wrap, then place the loaf pan back over the remaining semifreddo. Turn the whole thing upside down so that the semifreddo is now inside the pan. Remove the platter or cutting board, then seal in plastic wrap before returning the pan to the freezer. One warning: the semifreddo will be slightly icier when you slice it again, since it will have thawed once and been refrozen.

CHOCOLATE SEMIFREDDO

Makes about 8 servings

Chocolate lovers, look no further for the smoothest frozen dessert in the book. Always use high-quality chocolate—and choose the percent of cocoa solids, from semisweet (around 55 percent) to bittersweet (upwards of 70 percent), based on your taste.

> **1 cup cold heavy cream**
> **4 large egg yolks, at room temperature**
> **½ plus ⅓ cup sugar**
> **¼ cup whole milk**
> **6 ounces semisweet or bittersweet chocolate, finely chopped**
> **1 teaspoon vanilla extract**
> **2 large egg whites**
> **¼ teaspoon salt**
> **½ teaspoon cream of tartar**

1. Line a 1-quart (4 × 9 × 2¼-inch) loaf pan with plastic wrap and place it in the freezer while you prepare the components of the semifreddo.

2. Beat the cream in a medium bowl with an electric mixer at high speed until doubled in volume, airy and smooth, but not stiff at all. Set aside at room temperature away from the stove's heat.

3. Bring about 3 inches water to a boil in a large saucepan set over high heat. Reduce the heat so that the water simmers gently. Clean and dry the mixer's beaters.

4. Place the egg yolks and the ½ cup sugar in a medium bowl that will eventually fit securely over the saucepan with the simmering water. Beat with an electric mixer at medium speed off the heat until thick and smooth, about 1 minute. Then add the milk, place the bowl over the saucepan, and continue beating, scraping down the sides of the bowl with a rubber spatula to prevent the yolks from scrambling

at the edges, until the mixture is thick enough to make glossy little mounds when the beaters are turned off, raised out of it, and the mixture itself dribbles back into the bowl, about 6 minutes. Remove the bowl from the heat (but keep the water boiling). Stir in the chocolate and vanilla until smooth. Set aside.

5. Clean the beaters again. Place the egg whites, salt, and the remaining ⅓ cup sugar in another bowl, set it over the simmering water, and beat until foamy, about 1 minute. Add the cream of tartar and continue beating, scraping down the sides of the bowl with a clean rubber spatula, until thick and shiny, about like Marsh-mallow Fluff, about 3 minutes. Remove the bowl from the heat—be careful of the escaping steam—and beat until room temperature, about 2 minutes. (While doing so, you can turn off the heat under the saucepan.)

6. Fold about half the egg-white mixture into the chocolate mixture with a rubber spatula until smooth, then fold in the remainder of the egg-white mixture. Gently fold in the whipped cream just until there are no white streaks visible.

7. Remove the prepared loaf pan from the freezer and pour this mixture into it. Spread with a rubber spatula until smooth. Do not press down. Freeze until set, 6 to 8 hours. Wrap the pan in plastic wrap to prevent its contamination by freezer odors; store in the freezer for up to 2 weeks.

8. To serve, place the loaf pan upside down on a cutting board or a serving platter. Gently rock it back and forth until the semifreddo pops free, holding on to the plastic wrap to release the semifreddo. Remove the pan and all plastic wrap; slice the semifreddo into 1-inch-thick pieces to serve on individual plates.

EASY SEMIFREDDO

Makes about 8 servings

You may not win first prize for authenticity with this simplified frozen dessert, but you will end up with a no-cook version of the Italian classic. Consider this an easy introduction that will get raves from your friends and family.

> **2 cups cold heavy cream**
> **6 tablespoons confectioners' (or "powdered") sugar**
> **2 teaspoons vanilla extract**
> **One 7½-ounce jar Marshmallow Fluff or Marshmallow Cream**

1. Line a 1-quart (4 × 9 × 2¼-inch) loaf pan with plastic wrap and place it in the freezer while you prepare the components of this recipe.

2. Beat the cream and confectioners' sugar in a large, cold bowl with an electric mixer at high speed until the cream has doubled in volume and holds soft peaks when the beaters are stopped and pulled up. Beat in the vanilla and about a third of the Marshmallow Fluff, then fold in the remainder of the Fluff with a rubber spatula, using long arcs so as not to deflate the mixture.

3. Remove the prepared pan from the freezer and spoon in the creamy mixture, spreading it gently to the corners with a rubber spatula. Freeze until cold and set but still soft, 6 to 8 hours. Wrap in plastic wrap; store this way for up to 3 weeks.

4. To serve, turn the pan upside down on a cutting board or a serving platter. Gently wriggle it around, holding on to the plastic wrap, until the semifreddo comes loose and pops out. Remove the pan and any plastic wrap; slice the loaf into 1-inch-thick pieces and serve these on individual plates.

GRAND MARNIER SEMIFREDDO

Makes about 8 servings

There's no more elegant finish to a meal than this silky semifreddo that's spiked with a delicate orange liqueur from France.

> 1 cup cold heavy cream
> 4 large egg yolks, at room temperature
> 1 cup sugar
> ¼ cup Grand Marnier
> 2 teaspoons grated orange zest
> 2 large egg whites, at room temperature
> ¼ teaspoon salt
> ½ teaspoon cream of tartar
> ½ teaspoon vanilla extract

1. Line a 1-quart (4 × 9 × 2¼-inch) loaf pan with plastic wrap and put it in the freezer while you prepare the various pieces of this semifreddo.

2. Beat the cream in a medium bowl with an electric mixer at high speed until doubled in volume and creamy, not at all buttery. Set aside at room temperature away from the stove's heat.

3. Bring about 3 inches water to a boil in a large saucepan set over high heat; reduce the heat so the water simmers gently. Clean and dry the mixer's beaters.

4. Place the egg yolks and ½ cup of the sugar in a bowl that will eventually fit snugly over the saucepan with the simmering water. First, beat away from the heat at medium speed until thick and pale yellow, about 2 minutes. Then beat in the Grand Marnier and orange zest and place the bowl over the saucepan. Beat at medium speed, frequently scraping down the sides of the bowl to prevent any eggs from scrambling along the edges, until the mixture is thick enough to make firm little mounds when the beaters are turned off and pulled up out of it, about 7 minutes. Remove from the heat and cool at room temperature for 5 minutes.

5. Clean the beaters again. Place the egg whites, salt, and the remaining ½ cup sugar in a second bowl; set it snugly over the saucepan with the simmering water. Beat at medium speed until frothy, about 1 minute. Add the cream of tartar and continue beating at medium speed, scraping down the sides of the bowl with a clean rubber spatula, until silky and shiny, about 4 minutes. Remove the bowl from the heat (you can turn off the heat under the saucepan) and beat in the vanilla. Continue beating at medium speed until room temperature, about 2 more minutes.

6. Working quickly, fold half the egg-white mixture into the egg-yolk mixture with a rubber spatula until smooth, then fold in the remaining egg-white mixture. Fold in the whipped cream in gentle arcs so as to incorporate it fully without deflating the mixture.

7. Remove the prepared pan from the freezer and pour the mixture into it. Gently smooth it into the corners, creating an even surface across the top without pressing down. Freeze until set, 6 to 8 hours. Wrap the pan in plastic wrap to ward off freezer odors; the semifreddo can be stored this way for up to 2 weeks.

8. To serve, invert the pan onto a serving platter or cutting board; wriggle it gently back and forth until the semifreddo releases onto the platter or board. Remove the pan and all plastic wrap. Slice the semifreddo into 1-inch pieces and serve them on individual plates.

MOCHA SEMIFREDDO

Makes about 8 servings

This luxuriant semifreddo is best after it has "ripened" in your freezer for 24 hours—that is, after the chocolate and coffee have infused the creamy mixture with their flavors.

> 1 cup cold heavy cream
> 5 large egg yolks, at room temperature
> ½ cup plus ⅓ cup sugar
> ½ cup brewed espresso, or 2 tablespoons instant espresso powder dissolved in ½ cup hot water
> 1 ounce unsweetened chocolate, grated or finely chopped
> 1 large egg white, at room temperature
> ¼ teaspoon salt
> ¼ teaspoon cream of tartar
> 1 teaspoon vanilla extract

1. Line a 1-quart (4 × 9 × 2¼-inch) loaf pan with plastic wrap and place it in the freezer while you prepare the recipe.

2. Beat the cream in a medium bowl with an electric mixer at medium speed until doubled in volume and able to hold soft peaks when the beaters are turned off and lifted up. Set aside at room temperature, well away from the stove's heat.

3. Bring about 3 inches water to a boil in a large saucepan set over high heat. Reduce the heat so the water simmers gently. Clean and dry the mixer's beaters.

4. Place the egg yolks and the ½ cup sugar in a medium bowl that will fit snugly over the pan with the simmering water. Beat them off the heat at first until thick and pale yellow, about 1 minute. Scrape down the sides of the bowl with a rubber spatula and set the bowl over the saucepan with the simmering water; continue beating at medium speed, scraping the sides frequently, until thick and very satiny,

about 2 minutes. Beat in the espresso; continue beating until the mixture can make small mounds in the pan when the beaters are turned off and lifted out of it, about 4 more minutes. Remove the bowl from the heat (keep the water simmering in the saucepan) and fold in the chocolate with a rubber spatula until melted and smooth, about 1 minute. Set aside at room temperature for 5 minutes.

5. Meanwhile, clean and dry the beaters once again. Place the egg white, salt, and remaining ⅓ cup sugar in another clean bowl that will fit nicely over the saucepan with the simmering water. Beat at medium speed until foamy, then beat in the cream of tartar. Set the bowl over the saucepan and continue beating the mixture until smooth and shiny, scraping the sides of the bowl with a clean rubber spatula as necessary, about 2 minutes. Remove the bowl from the heat and beat in the vanilla. (You can turn off the heat under the saucepan.) Continue beating until room temperature, about 1 minute.

6. Working quite quickly, fold about half of the egg-white mixture into the egg-yolk mixture with a rubber spatula until smooth, then fold in the remaining egg-white mixture. Fold in the whipped cream just until no white streaks are visible.

7. Remove the prepared loaf pan from your freezer and pour this mixture into it, smoothing it out with a rubber spatula to fill the pan. Freeze until set and sliceable but nonetheless soft, 6 to 8 hours. Once the semifreddo is set, cover the pan tightly with plastic wrap; the semifreddo can be stored this way in the freezer for up to 2 weeks.

8. To serve, turn the loaf pan upside down on a serving platter or cutting board and gently wiggle it from side to side, holding down the plastic wrap, until the semifreddo comes free. Be gentle—you don't want to mush it out of shape. Pull off all the plastic wrap and cut into slices about 1 inch thick.

Nesselrode Semifreddo

Makes about 8 servings

Nesselrode pie is something of a New York City legend—a chestnut cream pie with candied fruit, popularized by Hortense Spier and her pre–World War II pie-baking business on West 94th Street. Spier made most of her pies for Manhattan's steak houses—and her Nesselrode was surely her best. Although no restaurants or bakeries now regularly make this classic in the city, here's a way to enjoy this retro treat in a velvety semifreddo.

> 1 cup cold heavy cream
> 4 large egg yolks, at room temperature
> One 14.8-ounce (420-gram) jar candied chestnuts in syrup, drained, chestnuts chopped, and ⅓ cup of the syrup reserved
> 2 tablespoons bourbon or brandy
> 1 large egg white, at room temperature
> ½ cup sugar
> ¼ teaspoon salt
> ¼ teaspoon cream of tartar
> ½ cup chopped glacéed or candied fruit, such as glacéed cherries or candied orange rind

1. Line a 1-quart (4 × 9 × 2¼-inch) loaf pan with plastic wrap and place it in the freezer while you make the semifreddo mixture.

2. Beat the cream in a medium bowl with an electric mixer at high speed until the cream doubles in volume and can hold soft peaks when the beaters are turned off and lifted up. Set aside at room temperature but well away from the stove's heat.

3. Bring about 3 inches water to a simmer in a large saucepan set over high heat. Reduce the heat so the water simmers gently. Clean and dry your mixer's beaters.

4. Place the egg yolks and the reserved syrup from the candied chestnuts in a medium bowl that will eventually fit snugly over the pan with the simmering water. First beat these two off the heat at medium speed until foamy and light, about 1 minute. Beat in the bourbon, then set this bowl over the saucepan—be careful of any escaping steam, which can give you quite a burn. Beat at medium speed until the mixture is thick and creamy and begins to hold its shape when the beaters are pulled up, about 4 minutes—occasionally, scrape down the sides of the bowl with a rubber spatula to prevent any egg yolks scrambling along its sides. Remove the bowl from the heat (keep the water simmering in the saucepan) and set aside at room temperature for 5 minutes.

5. Meanwhile, clean and dry the beaters once again. Place the egg white, sugar, and salt in a medium bowl that again will fit snugly over the pan with the simmering water. Beat at medium speed until foamy, about 1 minute. Add the cream of tartar, set the bowl over the saucepan, and beat at medium speed until marshmallowy and satiny, scraping down the sides of the bowl with a clean rubber spatula as necessary, about 3 minutes. Remove the bowl from the heat (turn off the heat under the simmering water) and beat until room temperature, about 2 minutes, perhaps less.

6. Working without delay, fold about half the egg-white mixture into the egg-yolk mixture with a rubber spatula until smooth, then fold in the remaining egg-white mixture. Fold in the chopped chestnuts and glacéed or candied fruit, then gently fold in the whipped cream, just until no white streaks are visible.

7. Remove the prepared loaf pan from the freezer and pour in this mixture, spreading it to the corners with a rubber spatula and thereby smoothing out the top without pressing down. Freeze until set, 6 to 8 hours. Cover the pan with plastic wrap to ward off freezer odors; store this way for up to 2 weeks.

8. To serve, turn the loaf pan upside down on a serving platter or cutting board, hold down the plastic wrap, and gently rock the pan from side to side to release the semifreddo. Remove the pan, pull off all the plastic wrap, and slice into 1-inch-thick pieces.

NOUGAT SEMIFREDDO

Makes about 8 servings

Imagine the texture of classic nougat—a soft confection of honey and almonds—only cold!

½ **cup sliced almonds**
1 **cup cold heavy cream**
3 **large egg yolks, at room temperature**
¼ **cup honey**
½ **teaspoon almond extract**
2 **large egg whites, at room temperature**
½ **cup sugar**
¼ **teaspoon salt**
½ **teaspoon cream of tartar**

1. Line a 1-quart (4 × 9 × 2¼-inch) loaf pan with plastic wrap and place it in your freezer while you prepare the various components of the semifreddo.

2. Toast the almonds in a skillet set over medium-low heat, stirring frequently until lightly browned and fragrant. Set aside at room temperature to cool.

3. Beat the cream in a medium bowl with an electric mixer at high speed until firm, light, airy, and smooth, but not buttery. Set aside at room temperature.

4. Bring about 3 inches water to a boil in a large saucepan set over high heat. Reduce the heat so the water simmers gently. Clean and dry the mixer's beaters.

5. Place the egg yolks and honey in a medium bowl that will fit securely over the saucepan with the simmering water. Beat away from the heat until light and thick, about 1 minute. Beat in the almond extract and place the bowl over the pan with the simmering water. Continue beating at medium speed for about 3 minutes, until the mixture will mound slightly when you pick the beaters up out of it—that is, the little dribblings from the beaters will form mounds on top of the mixture.

Remove the bowl from the heat (but keep the water simmering); set aside at room temperature for 5 minutes.

6. Meanwhile, clean and dry the beaters again. Place the egg whites, sugar, and salt in another medium bowl, set it securely over the pan with the simmering water, and beat at medium speed until frothy. Add the cream of tartar and continue beating until light, fluffy, and shiny, scraping the sides of the bowl occasionally with a clean, dry rubber spatula, about 4 minutes. Remove the bowl from the heat (you can turn off the heat under the saucepan) and beat until room temperature, about 2 more minutes.

7. Working efficiently, fold about half the egg-white mixture into the egg-yolk mixture with a rubber spatula until smooth, then fold in the remaining egg-white mixture. Fold in the toasted almonds, then the whipped cream, using large, gentle arcs so as not to deflate the mixture—however, there should be no white streaks visible when you're finished.

8. Remove the prepared pan from the freezer and pour in the mixture, spreading it out evenly in the pan with a rubber spatula without pressing down. Freeze until well chilled and firm enough to cut into slices, even if still soft and creamy, 6 to 8 hours. Cover the pan tightly with plastic wrap and store in your freezer for up to 2 weeks.

9. To serve, turn the loaf pan upside down onto a cutting board or serving platter; wiggle the pan from side to side, holding on to the plastic wrap to release the semifreddo. Take care—it's soft and you don't want to smoosh it. Remove the loaf pan and the plastic wrap, then slice the semifreddo into pieces about 1 inch thick.

Nutty Semifreddo

Makes about 8 servings

Use any of the nuts suggested for this treat. Serve the slices atop a little bed of chocolate sauce, if desired.

> 1 cup pecan pieces, walnut pieces, chopped skinned hazelnuts, or chopped unsalted pistachios
>
> ⅔ cup cold heavy cream
>
> 4 large egg yolks, at room temperature
>
> ¼ cup packed dark brown sugar
>
> 3 large egg whites, at room temperature
>
> 1 cup granulated sugar
>
> ¼ teaspoon salt
>
> ½ teaspoon cream of tartar

1. Preheat the oven to 350°F. While it's heating up, line a 1-quart (4 × 9 × 2¼-inch) loaf pan with plastic wrap and place it in the freezer to chill while you make this recipe.

2. Spread the nuts on a large baking sheet; bake, stirring frequently, until lightly browned and aromatic, about 7 minutes. Cool at room temperature for 10 minutes, then place them in a large food processor fitted with the chopping blade or a mini food processor and pulse until ground to the consistency of fine cornmeal, stopping the machine and rearranging larger pieces as need be. Set aside.

3. Beat the cream in a medium bowl with an electric mixer at high speed until doubled in volume and very creamy. Set aside at room temperature away from the heat.

4. Bring about 3 inches water to a boil over high heat in a large saucepan. Reduce the heat so that the water simmers gently. Clean and dry your mixer's beaters.

5. Place the egg yolks and brown sugar in a heat-safe bowl that will fit securely over the pan with the simmering water. Beat away from the heat at medium speed until thick and pale brown, about 1 minute. Place the bowl over the pan with the simmering water and continue beating, frequently scraping down the sides of the bowl with a rubber spatula, until the mixture will make little mounds when the beaters are stopped and pulled up out of it, about 4 minutes. Remove from the heat (keep the water simmering) and set aside at room temperature for 5 minutes.

6. Meanwhile, clean and dry the beaters again. Place the egg whites, granulated sugar, and salt in another bowl, set it securely over the pan with the simmering water, and beat at medium speed until frothy, about 1 minute. Add the cream of tartar; continue beating, scraping down the sides of the bowl with a clean, dry rubber spatula, until smooth, shiny, and silky, about 4 minutes. Remove the bowl from the heat (you can turn off the heat under the simmering water), add the ground nuts, and beat until the mixture is cooled to room temperature, about 1 minute.

7. Working quickly, fold about half the egg-white mixture into the egg-yolk mixture with a rubber spatula until smooth, then fold in the rest of the egg-white mixture. Fold in the whipped cream, using gentle strokes so as not to deflate it.

8. Remove the prepared pan from the freezer and pour in this mixture. Use a rubber spatula to spread the mixture gently but evenly in the pan. Freeze until firm and cold, 6 to 8 hours. Wrap the pan tightly in plastic wrap to protect the semifreddo from freezer odors. It can be stored this way in the freezer for up to 2 weeks.

9. To serve, invert the loaf pan onto a cutting board or a serving platter. Rap it gently a few times, holding on to the plastic wrap if possible, until the semifreddo comes free. Remove the pan and all plastic wrap. Slice the semifreddo into pieces about 1 inch thick and serve them on individual plates.

RICOTTA SEMIFREDDO

Makes about 8 servings

We wanted to create a frozen dessert that had the taste of cheesecake but also the silky texture of a classic semifreddo. This sumptuous treat is best served with a little fresh strawberry sauce on the side.

> ½ cup cold heavy cream
> 4 large egg yolks, at room temperature
> ½ cup plus ⅓ cup sugar
> 1½ cups whole-milk ricotta cheese, at room temperature
> 2 teaspoons vanilla extract
> 2 large egg whites, at room temperature
> ½ teaspoon cream of tartar

1. Line a 1-quart (4 × 9 × 2¼-inch) loaf pan with plastic wrap and place it in the freezer while you prepare the components of the semifreddo.

2. Beat the cream in a medium bowl with an electric mixer at medium speed until light and airy, about the consistency of thawed Cool Whip. Set aside at room temperature but away from the stove's heat.

3. Place about 3 inches water in a large saucepan and bring it to a boil over high heat. Reduce the heat so the water simmers gently. Clean and dry the mixer's beaters.

4. Place the egg yolks and the ⅓ cup sugar in a bowl that will fit snugly over the saucepan with the simmering water. Beat away from the heat at medium speed until thick and pale, about 1 minute. Place the bowl over the saucepan and continue beating, scraping down the sides of the bowl with a rubber spatula, until the mixture will make silky mounds when you turn off the beaters and pull them up out of it, about 3 minutes. Cool off the heat for 1 minute (maintain the water's simmer), then transfer the egg-yolk mixture to a food processor fitted with the chopping blade. Add the ricotta and vanilla; process until smooth. Return this mixture to the bowl you used to beat the egg yolks; set aside at room temperature for 5 minutes.

5. Meanwhile, clean and dry the beaters again. Place the egg whites and the remaining ½ cup sugar in another bowl that will fit over the simmering water as before. Set the bowl over the saucepan and beat at medium speed, scraping down the sides of the bowl with a clean rubber spatula, until frothy. Add the cream of tartar and continue beating until smooth and shiny, about 3 minutes. Remove the bowl from the heat (you can turn the heat off under the simmering water) and continue beating until the mixture is room temperature, about 2 more minutes.

6. Working quickly, fold half the egg-white mixture into the egg-yolk mixture with a rubber spatula until smooth, then fold in the remaining egg-white mixture. Gently fold in the whipped cream until there are no more white streaks.

7. Remove the prepared pan from the freezer and pour this mixture into it. Use a clean rubber spatula to smooth it out—gently, of course—and to get it to the corners of the pan. Freeze until cold and firm, 6 to 8 hours. Once the semifreddo's set, wrap the pan in plastic wrap to ward off freezer odors. The frozen dessert can be stored in the freezer like this for up to 2 weeks.

8. To serve, invert the loaf pan onto a cutting board or serving platter. Give it a rap or two against the hard surface so that the semifreddo will come loose and fall out. Remove the loaf pan and all plastic wrap. Slice the semifreddo into pieces about 1 inch thick and serve them on individual plates.

VANILLA SEMIFREDDO

Makes about 8 servings

This creamy semifreddo is best served with fresh berries or a few crunchy cookies. Or drizzle each plate with a little purchased caramel sauce.

> 1 cup cold heavy cream
> 4 large egg yolks, at room temperature
> ¾ cup sugar
> 1½ tablespoons vanilla extract
> 2 large egg whites, at room temperature
> ¼ teaspoon salt
> ½ teaspoon cream of tartar

1. Line a 1-quart (4 × 9 × 2¼-inch) loaf pan with plastic wrap and place it in your freezer to chill while you make the egg-and-cream mixture.

2. Beat the cream in a medium bowl with an electric mixer at high speed until doubled in volume and holds soft peaks when the beaters are turned off and lifted up. Set aside at room temperature, well away from the stove's heat.

3. Bring about 3 inches water to a boil in a large saucepan set over high heat. Reduce the heat so the water simmers gently. Clean and dry the beaters for your mixer.

4. Place the egg yolks and ¼ cup of the sugar in a bowl that will fit snugly over the pan with the simmering water. Beat away from the heat at medium speed until thick and pale yellow, about 1 minute. Set the bowl over the saucepan and continue beating until the mixture will make little mounds when the beaters are turned off, lifted up, and any mixture on them is allowed to dribble back into the pan, about 2 more minutes. Beat in the vanilla, then remove the bowl from the saucepan (do not turn off the heat under the pan) and set aside at room temperature for 5 minutes.

5. Meanwhile, clean and dry the beaters once again. Place the egg whites, salt, and the remaining ½ cup sugar in another bowl and fit it snugly over the saucepan with the simmering water. Beat at medium speed for 1 minute, until frothy. Add the cream of tartar and continue beating at medium speed, scraping down the sides of the bowl occasionally with a rubber spatula, until smooth, shiny, and satiny, about 3 minutes. Remove the bowl from the saucepan and continue beating off the heat until room temperature, about 1 more minute.

6. Fold about half the egg-white mixture into the egg-yolk mixture with a rubber spatula until smooth, then fold in the remaining egg-white mixture. Fold in the whipped cream gently, just to incorporate it without losing much of the volume.

7. Take the prepared loaf pan out of the freezer and pour this mixture into it. Spread the mixture gently to the corners with a rubber spatula. Return to your freezer and chill until cold and thick, for 6 to 8 hours. Once the semifreddo it set, cover the pan tightly with plastic wrap to ward off freezer odors; the semifreddo can be stored this way for up to 2 weeks.

8. To serve, turn the loaf pan upside down on a serving plate; hold the plastic wrap at the sides and lift off the pan, wiggling it from side to side. Pull the plastic wrap off the semifreddo and cut into slices about 1 inch thick.

ZABAGLIONE SEMIFREDDO

Makes about 8 servings

While other semifreddi may have a zabaglione-like mixture of cooked egg yolks and sugar, here's one made with the real thing. There's no egg-white mixture here, so the resulting texture's a little icier; but if you let it sit out a little before slicing, you'll find the creamy texture is well offset by the classic taste of this Italian creation.

6 large egg yolks, at room temperature
½ cup sugar
¼ cup sweet Marsala (see Note)
⅛ teaspoon salt
1½ cups cold heavy cream

1. Line a 1-quart (4 × 9 × 2¼-inch) loaf pan with plastic wrap and place it in your freezer while you prepare the zabaglione and whipped cream.

2. Bring about 3 inches water to boil over high heat in a medium saucepan. Reduce the heat so the water simmers gently.

3. Place the egg yolks and sugar in a medium bowl and beat with an electric mixer away from the heat until foamy and light, about 1 minute. Place the bowl over the saucepan of simmering water and beat in the Marsala and salt. Continue beating at medium speed, scraping down the sides of the bowl frequently with a rubber spatula, until the mixture mounds when you lift the beaters out of it, about 6 minutes. Remove from the heat (turn off the heat under the saucepan, too) and set aside at room temperature.

4. Clean and dry the mixer's beaters. Beat the cream at medium speed in a large bowl until doubled in volume and light, even if still loose, not stiff.

5. Fold the whipped cream into the egg-yolk mixture with a rubber spatula, taking care to incorporate it fully without deflating it completely.

6. Remove the prepared pan from the freezer and spread this mixture into it. Freeze until cold and set, 6 to 8 hours. Cover the pan tightly in plastic wrap to ward off freezer odors. The semifreddo can be stored this way in your freezer for up to 3 weeks.

7. To serve, let the pan stand at room temperature for 5 minutes, then turn it upside down onto a serving platter or a cutting board. Wiggle the pan a few times to release it from the semifreddo, then pull it away and take off all plastic wrap. Slice the semifreddo into pieces about 1 inch thick and transfer them to individual plates.

NOTE: This fortified Sicilian wine is available in sweet and dry varieties. Use only the former in this semifreddo. Store what's left, tightly stoppered, in the refrigerator for up to 1 month and serve it as a dessert wine at your next gathering.

Frozen Cakes, Pies, Mousses, and More

Frozen cakes and pies may well be the model American desserts. These make-ahead treats show up at potlucks, socials, and family gatherings all year long. Consider an ice cream cake a plan-ahead pleasure.

You might well consider an ice cream cake a plan-ahead pleasure. And while these desserts are certainly convenient and time-saving—there's no harried push to get dessert on the table after a big meal—some still do require the extra step of making gelato. Although we hope you occasionally go to that trouble for these show-stoppers, we always offer you the option of using store-bought ice cream. Just remember its quality will dramatically affect the finished dessert.

We can only think of two problems. A frozen chiffon or mousse is often made with raw eggs. For health reasons, we've always shied away from them. Toddlers, the elderly, and people with compromised immune systems should never eat them. But lately, pasteurized, in-the-shell eggs have begun showing up in our markets. While expensive, they're a boon for those who would like to make these treats without worry.

Frozen desserts are also prone to iciness. Gelati are less prone because of the high protein–fat ratio; sherbets, more so. Granite trade in it. But you don't want that toothache crunch in a chiffon pie. It doesn't help matters that most people nowadays own self-defrosting freezers. A modern convenience, no doubt—you never have to put in those great pots of steaming water and jackhammer the ice off the freezer walls while peas and chicken breasts melt in the sink. But frozen desserts, continually subjected to the fluctuating temperatures of self-defrosting units, naturally develop ice crystals over time.

The solution? While these are truly make-ahead treats, don't make them too far ahead. If you own a self-defrosting freezer, plan on eating your frozen cake or pie within 72 hours of its preparation. And always let the chiffon cakes and pies soften a few minutes at room temperature before serving.

In the end, you've got a terrific collection of frozen treats here, not just rehashed retro desserts. Besides new creations like Frozen S'mores Pie, we've updated the recipes considerably, using convenience products now and then, and adapting the tastes to more modern palates: less sweet, for one thing. We've also cut down on the whipped cream and thereby increased the natural flavors, whether they be lime, strawberry, or chocolate. That alone should keep you baking—or freezing—for a long time.

A Note About Pans

Many of these desserts are made in 8-, 9-, or 10-inch springform pans. The pans are measured on the diameter and have a latched side wall like a collar that fits into a groove along the bottom of the pan and locks into place. Make sure the side wall is indeed secure before you add any mousse or chiffon; otherwise, the wet mixture will leak out all over your freezer. Nonstick surfaces are helpful but not necessary. If your pans have this convenience, make sure you use approved cutlery and spatulas so you don't nick the coating and render the surface ineffectual.

One frozen cake here, the Pineapple Upside-Down Cake, is made in an 8-inch cheesecake pan. This traditional bakeware does not have a detachable side wall; it is a solid pan with 3- to 4-inch-high sides (i.e., much higher than a standard cake pan).

Frozen Banana Tofu "Cheesecake"

Makes 8 servings

This dairy-free dessert isn't a real cheesecake, of course. But once frozen and then softened for a few minutes, it has much the look and taste of the original—and is therefore the perfect frozen dessert for various dietary and religious restrictions. The toasted pecan crust adds a wonderful crunch.

> 2 cups pecan pieces
> 1 cup plus 2 tablespoons granulated sugar
> 2 cups vanilla soy milk
> ½ cup banana nectar
> ½ cup packed light brown sugar
> ¼ cup agar-agar flakes (see Note)
> 28 ounces firm silken tofu, such as Mori-Nu firm silken tofu
> 3 large ripe bananas, chopped
> 1 tablespoon lemon juice
> 1 tablespoon vanilla extract
> ¼ teaspoon salt

1. To make the crust, position a rack in the center of the oven and preheat the oven to 350°F. Spread the pecans on a baking sheet and toast them in the oven, stirring frequently, until lightly browned, about 5 minutes. Cool for 5 minutes.

2. Pour the nuts into a food processor fitted with the chopping blade, add the 2 tablespoons sugar, and process until finely ground, like cornmeal. Press this mixture evenly across the bottom and a little less than 1 inch up the sides of a 9-inch springform pan. Rather than doing it all at once, it helps to pour in about half the crust mixture, press it across the bottom as evenly as possible, then pour the rest of the mixture around the inner wall, right where the side meets the bottom, and gently press it into place along the sides. Place the pan with the prepared crust in the freezer while you prepare the filling.

3. Heat the soy milk, banana nectar, brown sugar, and the 1 cup granulated sugar in a large saucepan set over medium heat, stirring until the sugars dissolve. Stir in the agar-agar flakes and bring the mixture to a simmer. Reduce the heat and simmer gently, stirring all the while, until the agar-agar flakes dissolve, about 5 minutes. Remove from the heat and pour the mixture into a large bowl; chill in the refrigerator until slightly thickened, about 2 hours. (Alternatively, fill an even larger bowl with ice water and nestle the bowl with the soy milk mixture into it; stir constantly with a rubber spatula, particularly along the bowl's bottom and sides, until the consistency of a loose pudding, about 3 minutes.) Once the filling is set, remove the bowl from the refrigerator or ice bath while you prepare the tofu mixture.

4. Clean and dry the food processor's bowl and chopping blade. Add the tofu, bananas, lemon juice, vanilla, and salt; process until smooth, scraping down the sides of the bowl as necessary. Whisk this mixture into the soy-milk custard and pour into the prepared pan. Return to the freezer to chill until set, for at least 4 hours, or overnight. Once it's firm, cover the pan tightly with plastic wrap; the "cheesecake" can be stored this way for up to 2 weeks, although it will taste best within 48 hours of its being made.

5. To serve, run hot water over a flatware knife, wipe it dry, and run it along the inside of the pan, between the pan and the crust, taking care not to scratch the pan but also not to shred the crust. Unlatch the pan and remove the side collar. Place the "cheesecake" on a serving platter, let stand at room temperature for 5 minutes, then slice as you would a cake. We do not recommend refreezing the "cheesecake" once it's softened.

NOTE: Agar-agar flakes (also packaged as "agar flakes") are a seaweed-based setting agent used in Asian cooking. They're available in most gourmet markets, health-food stores, or Asian markets. The flakes must be heated to activate their enzymes. Agar-agar flakes make this "cheesecake" vegan, without the animal by-products in gelatin.

Customize it!
Substitute walnuts or hazelnuts for the pecans. Or substitute mango nectar for the banana nectar for a Tropical Tofu "Cheesecake."

FROZEN BAVARIAN CREAM PIE

Makes 8 servings

A Bavarian cream is a traditional cold dessert, something of a '50s dinner-party classic, made from custard and whipped cream, thickened with gelatin. Beaten egg whites are not customary, but we find their addition gives the custard a creamier consistency, a better match to the vanilla-cookie pie shell.

> 35 vanilla wafer cookies
> ⅔ cup plus 2 tablespoons sugar
> 5 tablespoons unsalted butter, melted and cooled
> One ¼-ounce package unflavored gelatin
> 1⅓ cups plus ¼ cup whole milk
> 4 large egg yolks, at room temperature
> 1 tablespoon vanilla extract
> ⅓ cup cold heavy cream
> 3 large egg whites, preferably from pasteurized eggs,
>   at room temperature
> ¼ teaspoon salt

1. To make the crust, crumble the cookies into a large food processor fitted with the chopping blade, add the 2 tablespoons sugar, and process until pulverized, stopping the machine as need be to arrange the larger chunks so they get ground up. With the machine running, pour the melted butter through the feed tube and continue processing just until the mixture begins to cohere into a mass. Place this ground mixture into a 9-inch pie plate, then press it gently but evenly across the bottom and sides until it comes up to the rim of the plate. Set in the freezer while you prepare the cream filling.

2. Sprinkle the gelatin over the ¼ cup milk in a small bowl; set aside to soften for 5 minutes.

3. Meanwhile, heat 1⅓ cups milk in a medium saucepan set over medium heat until small bubbles fizz along the pan's inner edge. Do not allow the milk to boil.

4. Beat the egg yolks and ⅔ cup sugar in a large bowl with an electric mixer at medium speed until pale yellow and fairly smooth, not grainy at all, about 4 minutes. With the mixer running at low speed, pour about half the warmed milk into the egg-yolk mixture, then beat or whisk this combined mixture back into the pan with the remaining warm milk. Stirring constantly, set the pan over low heat (use a second burner just now turned to low if you're working on an electric stove) and cook just until the mixture turns foamy and can coat the back of a wooden spoon, about 3 minutes. Remove the pan from the heat and stir in the vanilla and the softened gelatin mixture until dissolved. Strain through a fine-mesh sieve into a clean bowl and refrigerate until the mixture begins to thicken like a very loose pudding, about 45 minutes.

5. Clean and dry the mixer's beaters. Beat the cream in a medium bowl at high speed until doubled in volume, stiff, but still glossy, not buttery at all. Set aside at room temperature.

6. Clean and dry the beaters again. Beat the egg whites and salt at high speed until airy and firm but not dry.

7. Use a rubber spatula to fold the beaten egg whites into the chilled custard. Gently fold in the whipped cream, just until no white streaks are visible. Mound the mixture in the prepared pie shell and freeze for at least 4 hours or overnight. Once the pie is set, cover it with plastic wrap to ward off any freezer odors; the pie can be kept this way for up to 2 weeks. To serve, remove the plastic wrap, let stand at room temperature for 5 minutes, and slice into wedges.

Chocolate Chip Bavarian Cream Pie   Fold 1 cup mini chocolate chips into the beaten heavy cream before folding into the filling.

Coffee Bavarian Cream Pie   Reduce the milk to 1⅓ cups. Sprinkle the gelatin over ¼ cup room-temperature espresso or very strong coffee. Heat the remaining milk as directed.

Orange Bavarian Cream Pie Reduce the milk to 1⅓ cups. Sprinkle the gelatin over ¼ cup frozen orange juice concentrate, thawed. Heat the remaining milk as directed. Beat the heavy cream with 2 teaspoons finely grated orange zest.

Pineapple Bavarian Cream Pie Reduce the milk to 1⅓ cups. Sprinkle the gelatin over ¼ cup frozen pineapple juice concentrate, thawed. Heat the remaining milk as directed.

FROZEN BOMBE

Makes 6 servings

A classic bombe is a dome-shaped frozen dessert made with layered gelato, ice cream, or sherbet. It's a great centerpiece for any dessert buffet or a standout at your next family picnic. You can, of course, vary the flavors and colors of the layers to fit the season, holiday, or your preferences—from lower-fat sherbets to a blowout gelato extravaganza.

> **1 quart Chocolate Gelato (page 30), or purchased chocolate ice cream**
> **1 pint Vanilla Gelato (page 98), or purchased vanilla ice cream**
> **1 pint Raspberry Sherbet (page 130), or purchased raspberry sherbet**
> **6 slices purchased angel-food or sponge cake**

1. Line a 2-quart round bowl with plastic wrap, allowing enough excess to hang over the sides that it can later be folded over the top to seal the bombe in the freezer. Set aside.

2. Place the chocolate gelato or ice cream in a large bowl and soften it by gently mashing it with the back of a wooden spoon. Spread with a rubber spatula into the prepared bowl in an even layer, taking care not to mess up the plastic wrap but making an upside-down dome that extends to ½ inch below the bowl's rim. Set in the freezer for 1 hour.

3. Soften the vanilla gelato or ice cream as in step 2; spread it into the bowl, covering up the chocolate gelato or ice cream and creating a second, fairly thin, concave layer, again almost up to the bowl's rim. Return to the freezer for 1 hour.

4. Soften the raspberry sherbet as in step 2 and fill the center "hole" of the bombe with it.

5. Cover the top with angel-food or sponge cake, cutting some slices so that you can make an even layer across the bombe. (This will later be your base when you turn the thing upside down.) Pull the plastic wrap up and over the top, sealing the

bombe in the bowl. Freeze for at least 6 hours, or overnight. The bombe can be stored this way for up to 2 weeks.

6. To serve, peel back the plastic wrap, revealing the layer of cake. Turn the bowl upside down on a cutting board or serving platter. Dampen several paper towels with hot water, wring them dry, and wipe the bowl to soften the bombe a little. Rock the bowl back and forth, holding the plastic wrap against the cutting board or serving platter, until the bowl comes loose. Remove it and all plastic wrap. Let the bombe stand for 5 minutes at room temperature, then slice into wedges and serve.

To Turn a Bombe into a Baked Alaska

You will need a candy thermometer, which is designed to withstand the high heat of sugar syrups and comes not only with degree gradations, but with various markings to indicate the stages of sugar crystallization (soft ball, firm ball, hard ball, etc.). You can find candy thermometers at baking supply stores and most kitchenware stores.

> **4 large egg whites, at room temperature**
> **1 cup sugar**
> **3 tablespoons water**

1. Position a rack in the center of the oven and preheat the oven to 475°F. Place the egg whites and 2 tablespoons of the sugar in a large bowl and set aside while you prepare the sugar syrup.

2. Stir the remaining sugar (14 tablespoons sugar) and the water in a small saucepan set over medium heat until the sugar dissolves. Clip a candy thermometer to the inside of the pan, bring the mixture to a boil, and continue cooking without stirring until the mixture reaches 248°F, or firm-ball stage.

3. Meanwhile, beat the egg-white mixture with an electric mixer at high speed until shiny and stiff.

4. When the sugar syrup reaches 248°F, slowly drizzle it into the egg white mixture, beating all the while at low speed. Be careful of splatters—it's very hot. Beat until all the syrup has been added, then continue beating until cool, 5 to 7 minutes.

5. Unmold the bombe as directed on page 188, but this time onto a baking sheet. Spread the meringue over it with a rubber spatula, coating the whole thing down to the cake layer; seal the meringue against the cake, gently pressing it against the cake with a rubber spatula. Make little curlicues of meringue all over the bombe, as with a meringue pie.

6. Bake for about 3 minutes, or until lightly browned. Immediately remove the bombe from the baking sheet, transferring it to a serving platter with one or two large metal spatulas. Slice at once and serve.

Frozen Cheesecake

Makes 8 servings

Here's a creamy, traditional, frozen cheesecake, spiked with lemon, set in a graham-cracker crust. It freezes into two layers, a denser cheesecake with a sour cream–like topping. Check out the variations for lots of ways to customize it to your taste.

> 1⅓ cups graham cracker crumbs (either purchased or from about 10 whole graham crackers finely ground in a food processor)
> 1¼ cups plus ⅓ cup sugar
> 5 tablespoons unsalted butter, melted and cooled
> 1 pound cream cheese (do not use low-fat or fat-free), cut into chunks
> ⅔ cup sour cream (do not use low-fat or fat-free)
> 4 large egg yolks, at room temperature
> ¼ cup lemon juice
> 1 cup cold heavy cream
> 2 teaspoons vanilla extract

1. To make the crust, mix the graham cracker crumbs, ⅓ cup sugar, and the melted butter in a medium bowl until thoroughly moistened. Pour half this mixture into a 9-inch springform pan; gently press a crust across the bottom of the pan as evenly as you can. Then pour the rest around the inner rim of the pan's bottom; press about 1 inch up the sides of the pan, filling in gaps across the pan's bottom as well. Place in the freezer while you make the filling.

2. Beat the cream cheese in a medium bowl with an electric mixer at medium speed until soft, about 2 minutes. Add ½ cup sugar and continue beating at medium speed until light and creamy, about 2 more minutes. Scrape down the sides of the bowl and beat in the sour cream until smooth. Set aside.

3. Now make the zabaglione-like mixture that gives the cheesecake its creaminess. Bring about 2 inches water to a boil in a medium pan set over high heat; reduce the heat so the water simmers gently. Clean and dry the mixer's beaters. Place the egg yolks and the remaining ¾ cup sugar in a medium bowl that will fit securely over the pan with the simmering water. Beat away from the heat at medium speed until thick, about 1 minute, then beat in the lemon juice. Place the bowl over the simmering water and continue beating, scraping down the sides of the bowl, until foamy and thick, about 5 minutes. Remove the bowl from the heat and set aside to cool at room temperature for 10 minutes, stirring occasionally.

4. Clean and dry the beaters again. Beat the cream and vanilla in a second medium bowl until doubled in volume and stiff but still creamy.

5. Using a rubber spatula, gently fold the egg-yolk mixture into the cream cheese mixture until smooth. Then fold in the whipped cream, just until no white streaks are visible. Pour into the prepared crust, smoothing the batter to create an even top. Chill in the freezer until firm, for at least 4 hours or overnight. Once the cheesecake's set, cover the pan with plastic wrap. The cake can be stored this way for up to 2 weeks.

6. To serve, run hot water over a flatware knife or an offset spatula, dry it thoroughly, and then slide the knife between the pan and the crust, running it around the inside of the pan to release the cake without shredding the crust or scratching the pan. Unlatch the pan and remove the collar-like walls. Transfer the cake to a serving plate and slice as desired. We do not recommend refreezing the cheesecake once it's softened.

Customize it!

Substitute an equivalent amount of any of the following for the lemon juice: almond-flavored liqueur such as Amaretto, brandy, chocolate-flavored liqueur such as Godiva, coffee-flavored liqueur such as Kahlúa, hazelnut-flavored liqueur such as Frangelico, room-temperature espresso or very strong coffee, or vanilla-flavored liqueur such as Licor 43.

Once you substitute any of the above for the lemon juice, you can also fold in 1 cup of any of the following with the beaten heavy cream: chopped hazelnuts, chopped pecans, chopped walnuts, semisweet chocolate chips, shaved bittersweet chocolate, sliced almonds, or white chocolate chips.

Frozen Cherry Lime Rickey Chiffon Cake

Makes 8 servings

Originally, a rickey was a Prohibition-era cocktail, lime juice shaken with gin. In '50s America, it morphed into a soda-fountain drink made with seltzer, lime juice, and cherry syrup. Here's our homage to the sweet-shop masterpiece, done up in a frozen cake.

 24 vanilla-cream sandwich cookies

 3 tablespoons unsalted butter, melted and cooled

 1 quart Cherry Gelato (page 26), or 1 quart purchased cherry-vanilla ice cream

 One 6-ounce can frozen limeade concentrate, thawed to room temperature

 1 teaspoon unflavored gelatin

 1 cup cold heavy cream

 3 large egg whites, preferably from pasteurized eggs, at room temperature

 ¼ teaspoon salt

 ¼ teaspoon cream of tartar

1. To make the crust, crumble the cookies into a large food processor fitted with the chopping blade; pulse a few times, rearrange the large chunks, and then process until finely ground. With the machine running, pour the butter through the feed tube; continue processing just until the mixture starts to cohere into a mass. Place half this mixture in an 8-inch springform cake pan and press across the bottom to form an even crust; pour the rest along the inner rim and build the crust 1 inch up the sides of the pan, covering the bottom evenly and smoothly. Place in the freezer while you soften the gelato or ice cream.

2. Place the gelato or ice cream in a large bowl and soften it by repeatedly pressing against it with the back of a wooden spoon, just until it's spreadable. Spoon this

mixture evenly into the prepared cake pan and return it to the freezer to harden, for at least 2 hours. (The recipe can be made up to this point 2 days in advance.)

3. To make the chiffon filling, place ½ cup of the limeade concentrate in a small bowl and sprinkle the gelatin over the top; set aside to soften for 5 minutes.

4. Heat the remainder of the concentrate in a medium saucepan set over medium heat until steam rises from its surface. Do not let the mixture come to a simmer. Stir in the gelatin mixture, remove the pan from the heat, and continue stirring until the gelatin dissolves, about 30 seconds. Set aside at room temperature.

5. Beat the cream in a medium bowl with an electric mixer at high speed until doubled in volume but soft and wet, not dry and stiff. Set aside.

6. Clean and dry the mixer's beaters. Beat the egg whites and salt at medium speed in yet another bowl until foamy. Add the cream of tartar and continue beating until soft, slack peaks form off the beaters when they're turned off and lifted up.

7. Use a rubber spatula to fold the beaten egg whites into the limeade mixture. Then fold in the whipped cream, using gentle strokes so that the cream doesn't lose its volume. Pour into the prepared pan and freeze until firm, for at least 4 hours, or overnight. Once the cake's set, cover the pan with plastic wrap to seal it against freezer odors; the cake can be stored this way for up to 2 weeks.

8. To serve, run hot water over a thin knife, dry it off, then run the knife between the pan's inner edge and the crust to loosen the cake—take care not to scratch the pan or tear the crust: slower is better. Unlatch the pan and remove its side collar. Transfer the cake to a serving platter, let stand at room temperature for 5 minutes, and slice as desired. We do not recommend refreezing the chiffon cake after it's softened.

Customize it!
You can make a frozen lime chiffon cake with any flavor of gelato you prefer—among our favorites are Coconut Gelato (page 36), Lemon Gelato (page 57), Lime Gelato (page 59), or Raspberry Gelato (page 88).

FROZEN CHOCOLATE MOUSSE PIE

Makes 8 servings

If you've got a hankering for chocolate, this creamy mousse pie is sure to fix you up. It's indulgent, to be sure—but if you want to go over the top, serve a dollop of Vanilla Gelato (page 98) alongside it.

> 1⅓ cups graham cracker crumbs, purchased, or from about 10 whole graham
>   crackers pulverized in a food processor fitted with the chopping blade
> ¾ cup plus ⅓ cup sugar
> 2 tablespoons cocoa powder, sifted
> 6 tablespoons unsalted butter or margarine, melted and cooled
> 8 ounces semisweet or bittersweet chocolate, chopped
> ¾ cup cold heavy cream (see Note)
> 4 large egg yolks, at room temperature
> 3 tablespoons chocolate liqueur, such as Godiva
> 2 teaspoons vanilla extract
> 3 large egg whites, at room temperature
> ¼ teaspoon salt

1. Stir the graham cracker crumbs, ⅓ cup sugar, the cocoa powder, and melted butter in a medium bowl until very moist. Spoon this mixture into a 9-inch pie plate; press evenly across the bottom and up the sides, making it firm and even with the plate's rim without ever packing it down. Set in the freezer while you prepare the mousse.

2. Place the chocolate in the top half of a double boiler set over about 2 inches of simmering water. If you don't have a double boiler, place the chocolate in a bowl that fits snugly over a saucepan with a similar amount of simmering water. Stir until half the chocolate has melted, then remove the top half of the double boiler or the bowl from the heat—be careful of the roiling steam—and continue stirring off the heat until the chocolate has fully melted. Set aside to cool at room tem-

perature while you prepare the remainder of the recipe. (You can turn off the heat under the pan, but don't discard the water.)

3. Beat the cream in a medium bowl with an electric mixer at high speed until doubled in volume; the whipped cream should be firm but not dry. Set aside at room temperature, well away from the kitchen heat.

4. Wash and dry the mixer's beaters. Return the water in the saucepan to a simmer. Place the egg yolks, ¼ cup of the sugar, and the chocolate liqueur in a bowl that will fit snugly over the saucepan; beat at medium speed away from the heat, scraping down the sides of the bowl as necessary with a rubber spatula, until thick but pale yellow, about 2 minutes. Set the bowl over the pan with the simmering water and continue beating until the mixture makes visible little mounds when it drips off the beaters once they're turned off and lifted up. Remove from the heat (this time, keep the water simmering). Use a rubber spatula to fold in the melted chocolate and vanilla until smooth. Set aside.

5. Clean and dry the mixer's beaters again. Place the egg whites and salt in yet another bowl that will fit over the saucepan with the simmering water. Beat away from the heat until foamy, then add the remaining ½ cup sugar and set the bowl over the simmering water. Beat at high speed, scraping down the bowl with a clean rubber spatula, until satiny and smooth, a little more than 2 minutes. Remove the bowl from the heat (now turn off the heat under the water) and continue beating until room temperature, about 1 minute.

6. Using a clean, dry rubber spatula, fold about half this meringue-like egg-white mixture into the egg-yolk mixture until smooth, then fold in the remainder of the egg-white mixture. Fold in the whipped cream just until no white streaks are visible. Mound this mixture into the prepared pie shell. Return to the freezer and chill until firm, for at least 4 hours or overnight. After 4 hours, cover the pie with plastic wrap; it can stay in the freezer for up to 2 weeks. To serve, remove the plastic wrap and let the pie stand at room temperature for 5 minutes before slicing.

Customize it!
Stir ½ cup of any of the following into the filling with the beaten heavy cream: chocolate-covered espresso beans, chopped hazelnuts, chopped

pecans, chopped walnuts, mini marshmallows, mint chocolate chips, semisweet chocolate chips, or white chocolate chips.

NOTE: For an easier version, substitute 1½ cups nondairy whipped topping for the whipped cream; omit the step in which you beat the cream and simply fold the whipped topping into the chocolate mixture as you would the whipped cream. If you substitute melted margarine for the butter, the frozen mousse pie is dairy free, perfect for those with lactose-tolerance problems or after meat meals in a kosher home.

FROZEN GRASSHOPPER PIE

Makes 8 servings

This classic combination of crème de menthe and chocolate may have gotten its start as a cocktail, but it was turned into a pie through a clever Knox gelatin campaign in the late '50s. Our frozen version uses two luscious layers—one mint, the other chocolate—and stacks them in the classic chocolate-cookie crust.

> 20 chocolate sandwich cookies
> 1 cup plus 2 tablespoons (18 tablespoons) sugar
> 3 tablespoons unsalted butter, melted and cooled
> ⅔ cup whole milk
> 1 teaspoon unflavored gelatin
> 3 large egg yolks, at room temperature
> ¼ cup green crème de menthe
> 3 or 4 drops green food coloring, optional
> ½ cup cold heavy cream
> 3 large egg whites, at room temperature
> ¼ teaspoon salt
> ¼ teaspoon cream of tartar
> 2 ounces unsweetened chocolate, grated
> 1 teaspoon vanilla extract

1. Crumble the cookies into a large food processor fitted with the chopping blade, add the 2 tablespoons sugar, pulse a few times, then process until finely ground. With the machine running, pour the melted butter through the feed tube; continue processing until the mixture just starts to cohere into a mass. Turn off the machine and pour the chocolate-crumb mixture into a 9-inch pie plate. Gently press across the bottom and up the sides of the pie plate until the mixture is even with the rim. Do not press down hard—the point is to make an even crust, not paving stones. Place in the freezer while you make the filling.

2. Place ⅓ cup of the milk in a small bowl and sprinkle the gelatin over the top. Set aside to soften for 5 minutes.

3. Meanwhile, whisk the egg yolks and ⅓ cup sugar in a medium bowl until thick and creamy, about 2 minutes; set aside, too. Fill a very large bowl with ice water and set it aside as well. (If you have a double sink, you can create this water bath in one half of it.)

4. Heat the remaining ⅓ cup milk in a medium saucepan over medium heat until small bubbles pop up along the pan's inner edge. Do not allow the milk to come to a simmer. Stir in the gelatin mixture, remove the pan from the heat, and continue stirring until the gelatin has dissolved.

5. Whisk about half this warm milk mixture into the egg yolks, then whisk this combined mixture into the remaining milk mixture in the pan. Set the pan over low heat and cook, stirring constantly, until the mixture can coat the back of a wooden spoon, about 1 minute. Do not allow the mixture to come to a simmer. Stir in the crème de menthe and green food coloring, if using, until uniform. Nestle the bowl with the mint custard into the prepared ice-water bath. Stir with a rubber spatula, scraping the sides and bottom almost constantly, until thickened and somewhat gelatinous, about 3 minutes. Remove from the bath and set aside.

6. Whip the cream in a medium bowl with an electric mixer at high speed until doubled in volume but still soft and wet. Fold the whipped cream into the mint custard, then pour the mixture into the prepared pie shell. Place in the freezer and chill while you make the chocolate layer.

7. Bring about 2 inches water to a boil in a medium saucepan set over high heat; reduce the heat so the water simmers gently.

8. Thoroughly clean and dry your mixer's beaters. Place the egg whites and salt in a clean, dry medium bowl that will fit securely over the pan with the simmering water. Beat away from the heat at medium speed until foamy, then add the remaining ⅔ cup sugar and the cream of tartar, place the bowl over the pan, and beat at medium speed until thick, smooth, and satiny, scraping down the sides of the bowl as necessary with a clean rubber spatula, about 3 minutes. Beat in the chocolate and vanilla, then remove the bowl from the heat and continue beating at medium speed until room temperature, about 1 minute.

9. Spoon this chocolate mixture over the mint layer of the pie and return to the freezer to chill, for at least 4 hours or overnight. Once the pie's set, cover it with plastic wrap; it can be stored this way for up to 2 weeks. To serve, remove the plastic wrap and slice into wedges.

Frozen Brandy Alexander Pie Substitute ¼ cup brandy for the crème de menthe. Omit the green food coloring. Add 2 tablespoons sugar to the egg yolks.

FROZEN JELLY ROLL

Makes 8 servings

Although a jelly roll is a show-stopper, it's not hard to make—just work quickly to roll it up in the sugared towel once it comes out of the oven, while the cake's still hot and pliable. This one's an orange cake enfolding vanilla gelato, but you can customize it to your tastes by changing the flavor of the gelato at will. Be sure to clear out enough room in your freezer to store this cake on a baking sheet.

> 1 cup all-purpose flour
> 1½ teaspoons baking powder
> ¼ teaspoon salt
> ½ cup confectioners' (or "powdered") sugar
> 2 large eggs, at room temperature
> ¾ cup granulated sugar
> 2 tablespoons orange juice
> 2 tablespoons vegetable oil
> 3 tablespoons finely grated orange zest
> ½ teaspoon vanilla extract
> 1 quart Vanilla Gelato (page 98), or purchased vanilla ice cream
> ½ cup orange marmalade

1. Position a rack in the center of the oven and preheat the oven to 400°F. Line a 10 × 15-inch nonstick jelly roll pan with parchment paper and set aside. Whisk the flour, baking powder, and salt in a small bowl until the baking powder is evenly distributed; set aside as well. Finally, lay a large, clean kitchen towel on your work surface and dust it generously with the confectioners' sugar.

2. Beat the eggs and granulated sugar in a medium bowl with an electric mixer at medium speed until thick and pale yellow with no graininess whatsoever from undissolved sugar, about 4 minutes. Beat in the orange juice and oil, then the zest and vanilla extract. Scrape down the sides of the bowl and fold in the flour mix-

ture with a rubber spatula, just until moistened (the batter may still be grainy but there should be no pockets of unmoistened flour). Spoon this mixture into the prepared pan, taking care to spread it to the corners with a rubber spatula and even out its surface without ever pressing down.

3. Bake until lightly browned, about 10 minutes. A toothpick inserted into the center of the cake should come out dry. Remove the pan from the oven and immediately run a knife around the edges of the pan to loosen the cake. Cool for 1 minute, then set the pan's long edge parallel to the long edge of the prepared kitchen towel and quickly tip the pan over. Lift off the pan; leave the parchment paper attached to the cake. Beginning at one of the long sides of the towel, roll the cake up, using the towel as a guide but taking care not to get it stuck in the cake as you roll it. Don't press down but do make as compact a roll as you can. Set aside to cool for at least 20 minutes or up to 3 hours.

4. After the cake has cooled, soften the gelato or ice cream by placing it in a large bowl and pressing it with the back of a wooden spoon until spreadable, not melted.

5. Carefully unroll the towel, thereby unrolling the jelly roll. Remove the parchment paper and discard it. Using a rubber spatula, spread the marmalade evenly over the exposed, erstwhile-papered side of the cake, leaving a 1-inch border all the way around. Spoon the vanilla gelato or ice cream evenly over the marmalade and smooth it down, also leaving a 1-inch border. Roll up the jelly roll again (this time, without the towel, although you can use it as a guide and aid to lift the cake as you roll). Wrap the cake in plastic wrap, transfer to a baking sheet for support, and place in the freezer for at least 2 hours, or overnight. Once it's firm, you can remove the baking sheet but be careful of items in your freezer crushing the cake. The jelly roll cake can be stored in the freezer for up to 2 weeks. To serve, remove the plastic and slice the cake into oval sections a little more than 1 inch thick.

An Easier Version   Use one 16-ounce box angel-food cake mix. Stir 2 large egg yolks, lightly beaten, and 1 cup of any of the following into the mix before spreading the batter into the prepared pan and baking as directed: banana nectar, flavored soy milk, mango nectar, peach nectar, pineapple juice, or pineapple-orange-banana juice.

Frozen Key Lime Mousse Cake

Makes 8 servings

Here's a tart frozen cake that's great after any spicy meal, from Szechwan to Southwestern. While Key limes may be hard to track down, bottled Key lime juice is readily available in most supermarkets, sometimes in the soft-drinks aisle.

> 1½ cups purchased graham cracker crumbs, or about 12 whole graham
> crackers finely ground in a food processor to make 1½ cups crumbs
> ⅓ cup plus ¼ cup sugar
> 8 tablespoons (1 stick) unsalted butter, melted and cooled
> One ¼-ounce envelope unflavored gelatin
> 3 tablespoons cool water
> 1 cup cold heavy cream
> ¼ teaspoon salt
> ⅔ cup Key lime juice
> 2 teaspoons finely grated lime zest, preferably Key lime zest
> 4 large eggs, separated, preferably pasteurized eggs, at room temperature

1. To make the crust, stir the graham cracker crumbs, 2 tablespoons of the sugar, and the melted butter in a large bowl until moist and dense, then gently press half this mixture into the bottom of a 10-inch springform pan, making as even a crust across it as you can. Sprinkle the remainder of the crumb mixture around the inner rim where the side meets the bottom and press the crust up the sides by about 1 inch, filling in any gaps along the bottom crust of the pan. Place in the freezer while you prepare the mousse filling.

2. Sprinkle the gelatin over the water in a small bowl or teacup; soften for 5 minutes. Fill a very large bowl halfway full of ice water and set aside as well. (If you have a double sink, you can use one side to make this ice-water bath.)

3. Beat the cream in a medium bowl with an electric mixer at high speed until doubled in volume, creamy, and firm without being stiff. Set aside at room temperature, well away from the heat.

4. Clean and dry the beaters. Beat the egg whites, 2 tablespoons of the sugar, and the salt in a second medium bowl until slack peaks form at the point in the mixture where the shut-off beaters are lifted out of it, about 3 minutes. Set aside as well.

5. Stirring constantly, heat the lime juice, zest, and the remaining ⅓ cup sugar in a medium saucepan set over medium heat just until the sugar dissolves. Do not bring the mixture to a simmer. Add the gelatin mixture, remove the pan from the heat, and stir until dissolved, about 20 seconds.

6. Whisk the egg yolks in a second medium bowl until foamy and creamy, then slowly whisk in the lime juice mixture, adding just a little at first to temper the eggs as you whisk, then adding more as the eggs incorporate into the mixture. Place this bowl in the ice-water bath you've prepared and continue whisking until the mixture is cool and starts to thicken, about 1 minute.

7. Using a rubber spatula, fold the beaten egg whites into the egg-yolk mixture, then fold in the whipped cream. Pour into the prepared springform pan, taking care not to dislodge the crust (it may help to spoon in the first bit, just to get it even across the bottom). Return the pan to the freezer and chill until firm, at least 4 hours or overnight. Once it's set, wrap the pan in plastic wrap to ward off freezer odors.

8. To unmold, run hot water over a flatware knife, dry it thoroughly, and then run this knife around the inner edge of the pan, thereby loosening the cake without breaking up the crust or scratching the pan. Unlatch the springform pan's side collar, remove it, and place the cake on a serving platter. Let stand at room temperature for 5 minutes before slicing.

Frozen Lemon Mousse Cake   Substitute lemon juice and finely grated lemon zest for the lime juice and lime zest.

Frozen Margarita Mousse Cake   Substitute tequila for the water used to soften the gelatin. Substitute finely grated orange zest for the lime zest.

Frozen Layer Cake

Makes 10 servings

Our version of the traditional ice cream cake is made with alternating layers of strawberry gelato (or purchased strawberry ice cream) and banana cake, which is a little denser than the standard, springy variety but a better foil for the copious amounts of gelato or ice cream. And what's the point of an ice cream cake that doesn't have copious amounts of ice cream? (See the variations below for lots of options and many more flavor combinations.)

> Nonstick spray
> 1½ cups all-purpose flour, plus additional for the pans
> ½ teaspoon baking powder
> ½ teaspoon baking soda
> ½ teaspoon salt
> 8 tablespoons (1 stick) unsalted butter, cut into chunks but still cool
> 1 cup sugar
> 2 large eggs, at room temperature
> ½ cup sour cream (regular or low-fat, but not fat-free)
> 2 large ripe bananas, well mashed
> 1 tablespoon vanilla extract
> ½ gallon Strawberry Gelato (page 94; make 2 quarts, a double recipe);
>   or ½ gallon purchased strawberry ice cream or frozen yogurt, softened
> ½ cup cold heavy cream, beaten with ¼ cup confectioners' (or "powdered")
>   sugar until doubled in volume and stiff, or 1 cup nondairy whipped
>   topping, optional
> 8 fresh strawberries, thinly sliced

1. Position a rack in the center of the oven and preheat the oven to 350°F. Spray two 9-inch round cake pans with nonstick spray, put a dollop of flour in each, and tap the pans along the edges, tilting them this way and that, until the sides and bot-

toms have a thin coating of white flour. Discard any excess flour; set the pans aside. Whisk the 1½ cups flour, baking powder, baking soda, and salt in a medium bowl; set aside as well.

2. Beat the butter in a large bowl with an electric mixer at medium speed until creamy and light, about 2 minutes. Scrape down the sides of the bowl with a rubber spatula, add the sugar, and continue beating until fluffy, with only sporadic grains of sugar detectable, about 2 more minutes. Beat in the eggs one at a time, making sure the first is fully incorporated before adding the second. Scrape down the sides of the bowl, then beat in the sour cream, banana, and vanilla until smooth.

3. Turn off the beaters and add the flour mixture. Beat at low speed just until incorporated. Do not overbeat. Divide the batter evenly between the two prepared cake pans, taking care to smooth it without pressing down.

4. Bake until a toothpick inserted in the center of one of the cakes comes out clean, 25 to 28 minutes. Transfer to a wire rack and cool for 5 minutes. Remove the cakes by topping a pan with a large plate, inverting the two together, gently tapping or shaking the cake loose, removing the pan, and reinverting the plate onto a wire rack. Repeat with the other cake layer. Cool completely, about 2 hours. If the tops of the cake layers are rounded, slice them off with a long, thin knife so each is perfectly flat.

5. Meanwhile, wash and dry the cake pans; line them each with plastic wrap. Mound half the gelato or ice cream into each pan (i.e., 1 pint in each); spread smooth with a rubber spatula. If you fold the plastic over the tops of the layers, you can use the other pan to compress a nice layer: set one pan on top of the other and press down lightly. Place the pans in the freezer until the gelato or ice cream is firm, about 1 hour.

6. Slip one of the cake layers onto a serving platter. Unmold one of the gelato or ice cream layers, gently pulling it out of the pan by the plastic wrap. Invert it on top of the cake layer and pull off the plastic wrap. Top with the other layer of cake, then the other layer of gelato or ice cream. If desired, the cake can be returned to the freezer for up to 8 hours. Cover loosely in plastic wrap to protect it from freezer odors.

7. To serve, take off the plastic wrap if it's been stored in the freezer and spread the whipped cream or nondairy whipped topping across the top of the cake. Decorate with sliced strawberries, perhaps placing them in rings around the upper edge of the cake and then mounding the rest in the center. Cut with a cake knife or other thin knife that's been dipped in hot water, then wiped dry.

Customize it!

For an easier version, use a boxed cake mix of any flavor you desire, from orange to lemon, chocolate to strawberry.

There's also a seemingly endless list of gelati (or purchased ice cream) that would work as a substitute for the strawberry. Some of our favorites include Banana Gelato (page 18), Blueberry Gelato (page 22), Blueberry Sherbet (page 109), Hazelnut Gelato (page 52), or Stracciatella (page 92). In these cases, replace the sliced strawberries on top with a matching ingredient for the gelato: sliced bananas, blueberries, chopped hazelnuts, or chocolate chips.

Or use a boxed cake mix and pair it with a matching gelato flavor—for example, orange cake with Orange Gelato (page 71) or Orange Sherbet (page 121); lemon cake with Lemon Gelato (page 57) or Lemon Sherbet (page 116); chocolate cake with Chocolate Gelato (page 30).

Frozen Mississippi Mud Pie

Makes 8 servings

The nonfrozen original of this Southern favorite was a recipe developed by Nabisco, a way to use Oreo cookies in a pie crust. We've preserved that original crust in our frozen version but used a combination of espresso and chocolate gelato for an ice cream lover's grail.

25 chocolate cream sandwich cookies, such as Oreos

2 tablespoons granulated sugar

5 tablespoons unsalted butter, melted and cooled

1 pint Espresso Gelato (page 44), or 1 pint purchased coffee ice cream (see Note)

½ cup purchased hot fudge sauce, at room temperature or warmed just until spreadable

1 pint Chocolate Gelato (page 30), or 1 pint purchased chocolate ice cream (see Note)

¼ cup purchased caramel sauce, at room temperature

1½ cups cold heavy cream

¼ cup confectioners' (or "powdered") sugar

¼ cup cocoa powder, sifted

1 teaspoon vanilla extract

1. To make the crust, pulverize the cookies and granulated sugar in a large food processor fitted with the chopping blade, turning the machine off occasionally to arrange large chunks so they get ground up. With the machine running, pour the butter through the feed tube; process just until the mixture begins to cohere. Gently press into the bottom and sides of a 9-inch pie plate, inching the crust up the sides until it's even with the plate's rim. Do not compact the crust—just press it lightly into place. Chill in the freezer for 1 hour.

2. Place the espresso gelato or the coffee ice cream in a large bowl and soften it by mashing against it with the back of a wooden spoon, just until it's spreadable. Spoon into the bottom of the pie plate and spread with a rubber spatula, taking care not to disturb the crust but making an even layer of gelato or ice cream. Drizzle the hot fudge sauce evenly over the top—you can spread it gently with a rubber spatula, if you desire. Place the pie back in the freezer and chill for 1 hour.

3. Soften the chocolate gelato or ice cream as you did in step 2, then spread an even layer over the espresso gelato and fudge sauce with a rubber spatula. Drizzle the caramel sauce over the top—again, you can spread it evenly over the top with a rubber spatula. Chill in the freezer for 1 hour.

4. Beat the cream in a large bowl with an electric mixer at high speed until foamy. Add the confectioners' sugar, cocoa powder, and vanilla; continue beating until soft, droopy peaks form at the point where the switched-off beaters are lifted out of it. Spread this whipped cream gently over the top of the pie. Return to the freezer and chill until set, at least 4 hours or overnight. After 4 hours, wrap the pie in plastic wrap to prevent its picking up freezer odors; it can be stored this way for up to 2 weeks. To serve, remove the plastic wrap and let the pie stand at room temperature for 5 minutes before slicing.

NOTE: The gelati recipes in this book make 1 quart—either make the whole recipe and use half of it, or divide the recipe in half and make a smaller batch in your ice cream machine. (Use 3 large egg yolks for the espresso gelato and 2 for the chocolate.) A smaller batch, however, will allow more air to get whipped into the custard because there's more head room in the machine.

FROZEN PEANUT BUTTER PIE

Makes 10 servings

It's hard to beat a frozen pie that's like a peanut-butter-marshmallow-fluff-and-jelly sandwich. A diet buster? Sure to make everyone's don't-dare-eat-this list? We hope so. Cut small pieces and throw caution to the wind.

> **16 peanut butter cream sandwich cookies, such as Nutter Butter cookies**
> **4 tablespoons (½ stick) unsalted butter, melted and cooled**
> **1 cup cold heavy cream**
> **2 teaspoons vanilla extract**
> **1½ cups creamy peanut butter**
> **One 14-ounce can sweetened condensed milk**
> **One 7½-ounce jar Marshmallow Fluff or Marshmallow Cream**
> **2 tablespoons grape jelly**
> **2 tablespoons salted peanuts, chopped**

1. To make the crust, crumble the peanut butter sandwich cookies into a large food processor fitted with the chopping blade. Pulse a few times to break them up, rearrange the chunks, then process until pulverized. With the machine running, pour the butter through the feed tube and process until moist and finely ground. Pour into a 9-inch pie shell and press gently but evenly across the bottom and up the sides. Place in the freezer while you prepare the pie's filling.

2. Beat the cream and vanilla in a medium bowl with an electric mixer at high speed until doubled in volume and firm, even if still soft, not dry. Set aside at room temperature.

3. Clean and dry the mixer's beaters. In a second bowl, beat the peanut butter and sweetened condensed milk at medium speed until smooth. Scrape down the sides of the bowl with a rubber spatula, then beat in the Marshmallow Fluff until silky. Remove the beaters and fold in half the whipped cream with a rubber spatula, then gently fold in the remainder of the whipped cream, taking care not to lose its

volume but nonetheless incorporating it fully. Pour the mixture into the prepared pie shell, mounding it high.

4. Place the jelly in a small bowl and beat it with a fork to soften it slightly. Drizzle over the top of the pie. Sprinkle the chopped peanuts over the pie as well. Return it to the freezer and chill until set, at least 4 hours or overnight. Once it's firm, cover the pie loosely with plastic wrap; it can be stored this way for up to 2 weeks. To serve, remove the plastic wrap and slice as desired.

Frozen Halvah Pie Substitute tahini (sesame paste) for the peanut butter.

Customize it!

Substitute any of the following for the peanut butter: almond butter, cashew butter, chocolate-hazelnut spread such as Nutella, crunchy peanut butter, hazelnut butter, or honey-roasted peanut butter.

FROZEN PINEAPPLE UPSIDE-DOWN CAKE

Makes 8 servings

Here's a frozen version of that all-American favorite, designed to make a light, bracing hit on a summer day.

> One 20-ounce can pineapple rings in heavy syrup, drained, syrup reserved
> 12 maraschino cherries
> One ¼-ounce package unflavored gelatin
> 1¼ cups whole milk
> 6 large egg yolks, at room temperature
> ¾ cup packed light brown sugar
> 2 tablespoons granulated sugar
> 2 teaspoons vanilla extract
> 1¼ cups cold heavy cream
> 3 large egg whites, preferably from pasteurized eggs, at room temperature
> ¼ teaspoon salt
> One 10- to 12-ounce purchased pound cake

1. Line an 8-inch cheesecake pan (see page 181) with plastic wrap, pressing it into the corners but keeping the wrap as tight and wrinkle free as possible. Leave enough excess hanging over the edges that it can later be folded over to cover the pan.

2. Place 6 pineapple rings in the bottom of the pan, one at the center and the other five surrounding it (reserve the other rings for another use). Place two cherries in the open center of each pineapple ring. Set aside.

3. Pour ⅓ cup of the reserved pineapple syrup into a small bowl; sprinkle the gelatin over the top. Set aside to soften while you prepare the other components of the cake.

4. Heat the milk in a medium saucepan set over medium heat until small bubbles pop up around the pan's inner rim. Adjust the heat so the milk stays this hot without boiling.

5. Beat the egg yolks, brown sugar, and granulated sugar in a medium bowl with an electric mixer until pale brown, thick, and fairly smooth, about 5 minutes. At low speed, beat in about half the warmed milk until smooth, then beat this combined mixture back into the pan with the remaining milk. Immediately reduce the heat to low—if you're using an electric stove, move the pan to a second burner turned just now to low. Cook, stirring constantly, until the mixture thickens and can coat the back of a wooden spoon, about 3 minutes. Stir in the vanilla and the gelatin mixture until dissolved, about 10 seconds. Strain through a fine-mesh sieve into a large bowl and chill in the refrigerator until cool and somewhat set, stirring once in a while, about 2 hours. (Alternatively, you can fill an even larger bowl with ice water and nestle the bowl with the chiffon in it; stir constantly with a rubber spatula, especially along the bowl's bottom and sides where it first firms up, until viscous and gelatinous, but not yet fully set, about 3 minutes.)

6. Clean and dry your mixer's beaters. Beat the cream in a large bowl at high speed until firm and luscious. Set aside.

7. Clean and dry the beaters again. Beat the egg whites and salt in another bowl at high speed until stiff but not dry.

8. Use a rubber spatula to fold the beaten egg whites into the egg-yolk mixture until smooth, then gently fold in the whipped cream until no white streaks are visible. Pour half this mixture into the prepared cheesecake pan, taking care not to mess up the plastic wrap on the pan's sides.

9. Slice the pound cake into ½-inch pieces and cover the layer of chiffon with some of them, breaking them to fit evenly across the surface. Sprinkle the cake with 2 tablespoons of the reserved pineapple syrup. Spoon the remainder of the chiffon into the pan, leveling it off with a rubber spatula. Top with more pound cake slices, forming a sealed top layer for the cake. Bring the excess plastic wrap up from the sides and cover tightly. Set in the freezer to firm up, for at least 4 hours or overnight. The cake can be stored this way for up to 2 weeks, although it will taste best within 48 hours of its being made.

10. To serve, turn the cake pan upside down on a cutting board or a serving platter. Run hot water over a few paper towels, wring them dry, then wipe the outside of the cake pan to loosen the cake inside. Rock the pan back and forth, holding the plastic wrap against the cutting board or serving platter, until the pan comes free. Remove it and all plastic wrap. Slice the cake as desired.

Frozen Apricot Upside-Down Cake Substitute one 20-ounce can apricot halves in syrup for the pineapple rings. Reserve the syrup and use as indicated. Place the apricot halves in the bottom of the pan, then place the cherries around them.

FROZEN RASPBERRY CHIFFON CAKE

Makes 8 servings

The difference between a mousse and a chiffon is all texture—a mousse is airier, thanks to more beaten egg whites and perhaps gelatin; a frozen chiffon, a little icier but more refreshing. Here, that bracing chiffon makes a cake just right for an evening out on the patio or a night around the fire.

> 50 thin chocolate wafer cookies
>
> 1¼ cups plus 3 tablespoons sugar
>
> 8 tablespoons (1 stick) unsalted butter, melted and cooled
>
> 3 cups fresh raspberries (about 1½ pints), or 3 cups frozen raspberries, thawed (around 17 ounces)
>
> ¼ teaspoon salt
>
> One ¼-ounce package unflavored gelatin
>
> ⅓ cup raspberry or cranberry juice
>
> 1½ cups cold heavy cream
>
> 5 large eggs, preferably pasteurized eggs, separated, at room temperature

1. To make the crust, place the wafers and 3 tablespoons sugar in a large food processor fitted with the chopping blade; process until pulverized, rearranging any large pieces so they can be crushed up. With the machine running, pour the butter through the feed tube; process just until moist. Pour half the mixture into a 9-inch springform pan and gently press a crust across the pan's bottom. Pour the remainder of the crust mixture around the inner rim of the pan and gently build the crust about halfway up the sides, making sure that the bottom is well coated. Do not compact the crust into place. Place in the freezer while you prepare the chiffon.

2. To make the filling, place the raspberries in a fine-mesh sieve set over a medium bowl; press them against the mesh with the back of a wooden spoon, thereby letting the pulp fall into the bowl while keeping the seeds in the sieve. You may need

to ball up the mixture a few times, wiping it across the mesh to get it going in a new direction, so you can get the most amount of juice from the berries. Discard the solids, stir the salt into the puree, and set aside.

3. Sprinkle the gelatin over the raspberry or cranberry juice in a small bowl; set aside to soften for 5 minutes.

4. Place the cream in a medium saucepan and set it over medium heat until small bubbles appear around the inner edges of the pan; reduce the heat so the cream does not come to a simmer.

5. Meanwhile, beat the egg yolks and 1 cup sugar in a medium bowl with an electric mixer at medium speed until pale yellow and thick, about 2 minutes. Beat in about a third of the heated cream, then stir this combined mixture back into the saucepan with the remaining cream. Reduce the heat to low and cook, stirring constantly, just until the mixture can coat the back of a wooden spoon, about 3 minutes.

6. Remove the pan from the heat and whisk in the gelatin until it dissolves. Then whisk in the raspberry puree. Place in the refrigerator and chill until slightly thickened, about 1 hour.

7. Now clean and dry the mixer's beaters. Beat the egg whites and the remaining ¼ cup sugar in a clean, dry bowl until they form airy, soft peaks when the beaters are turned off and lifted up. Using a rubber spatula, fold these whites into the chilled raspberry mixture until no white streaks are visible—fold gently so as to keep the volume of the mixture. Pour into the prepared pan with the chocolate-cookie crust. Freeze in the freezer until firm, for at least 6 hours, or overnight. Once the cake's set, cover the springform pan in plastic wrap to keep any freezer odors out; it can be stored this way for up to 2 weeks, although it will taste best within 2 days of its being made.

8. To serve, run hot water over a flatware knife, wipe it dry, and run it around the inside of the pan, taking care to sever the crust from the pan and not break up the crumbs too much. Unlatch the pan and remove the side. Transfer the cake to a serving platter and let it stand at room temperature for 5 minutes before cutting.

Frozen Peach Melba Chiffon Cake   Spread 1 quart Peach Gelato (page 73) or purchased peach ice cream evenly in the pan on top of the chocolate-cookie crust, then place in the freezer while you make the chiffon. Pour the chiffon on top of the gelato.

Frozen Raspberry Cream Chiffon Cake   Spread 1 quart Vanilla Gelato (page 98) or purchased vanilla ice cream evenly in the pan on top of the chocolate-cookie crust, then place in the freezer while you make the chiffon. Pour the chiffon on top of the gelato.

Frozen Raspberry Mint Chiffon Cake   Spread 1 quart Mint Gelato (page 67) or purchased mint ice cream evenly in the pan on top of the chocolate-cookie crust, then place in the freezer while you make the chiffon. Pour the chiffon on top of the gelato.

Frozen S'mores Pie

Makes 10 servings

This ultra-rich pie is a cold reinterpretation of the campfire favorite. The filling is much like melted marshmallows, placed on a graham-cracker crust slathered with hot fudge sauce. The caramel sauce on top is for sheer excess.

> 1⅓ cups purchased graham cracker crumbs, or about 10 whole graham crackers, finely ground in a food processor to produce 1⅓ cups crumbs
>
> 1 cup plus 3 tablespoons sugar
>
> 5 tablespoons unsalted butter, melted and cooled
>
> ¾ cup purchased hot fudge sauce, placed in a bowl and softened in a microwave for 10 to 15 seconds, just until pourable, then cooled
>
> 3 large eggs, separated, at room temperature
>
> ¼ teaspoon salt
>
> ¼ teaspoon cream of tartar
>
> 1 tablespoon vanilla extract
>
> 3 tablespoons purchased caramel sauce

1. Stir the graham crackers, 3 tablespoons sugar, and melted butter in a medium bowl until moist. Gently press into a 9-inch pie plate, evenly coating the bottom and sides with a crust, up to the plate's rim. Slowly drizzle the hot fudge sauce over the crust; use a rubber spatula to make an even layer, taking care not to dislodge the cookie crumbs. Place in the freezer while you prepare the filling.

2. To make the zabaglione-like mixture that is the base for the filling, bring about 3 inches water to a boil in a medium saucepan set over high heat; reduce the heat so the water simmers gently. Place the egg yolks and ⅓ cup sugar in a medium bowl that will fit securely over the pan with the simmering water. Beat away from the heat with an electric mixer at medium speed until thick and pale, about

2 minutes. Then place the bowl over the pan and continue beating at medium speed until quite thick, like mayonnaise, about 2 minutes. Remove the bowl from the heat (maintain the water's boil) and set aside at room temperature for 10 minutes.

3. Now make the cooked meringue that provides the marshmallowy texture. Thoroughly clean and dry the mixer's beaters. Place the egg whites and salt in a second bowl that will also fit securely over the simmering water; beat at medium speed away from the heat until foamy. Add the remaining ⅔ cup sugar and the cream of tartar; place the bowl over the pan. Beat at high speed until thick and shiny, scraping down the sides of the bowl as necessary, about 3 minutes. Remove the bowl from the heat and beat in the vanilla. Continue beating until room temperature, about 1 minute.

4. Use a rubber spatula to fold the egg-white mixture into the egg-yolk mixture. Mound into the prepared pie shell. Drizzle the caramel sauce over the pie. Freeze until set, for at least 4 hours or overnight. Once it's firm, loosely cover with plastic wrap; the pie can be stored this way for up to 2 weeks. To serve, remove the plastic wrap and slice as desired.

Frozen Soufflé

Makes 6 servings

Here's one of the classics: a light, lemony, refreshing, frozen soufflé. It may be a little retro, a little bit of '50s entertaining nostalgia, but we guarantee it'll be a hit at your holiday parties or weekend get-togethers. Serve it with the Fresh Berry Sauce (recipe follows).

> 8 tablespoons (1 stick) unsalted butter, cut into pieces
> 1 cup sugar
> ⅔ cup lemon juice
> 3 tablespoons finely grated lemon zest
> 5 large eggs, preferably pasteurized eggs, separated, plus 3 large egg yolks, at room temperature
> ¼ teaspoon salt
> 1 cup cold heavy cream (see Note)

1. Cut a piece of wax paper or parchment paper to use as a collar on a 1-quart soufflé dish. The collar should extend at least 3 inches above the rim of the dish with a 2-inch overlap at the seam. Thread three or four straight pins through the seam to close the collar against the dish, or staple the collar closed at the seam; in any case, make sure it fits tightly against the dish. Secure the collar against the outside of the dish with one or two rubber bands. Set aside.

2. Melt the butter in the top half of a double boiler set over about 2 inches of simmering water in the double boiler's bottom half, all placed over medium heat. Or melt the butter into a large bowl that fits snugly over a medium saucepan with a similar amount of simmering water. Whisk in the sugar, lemon juice, and lemon zest until the sugar dissolves. Reduce the heat so the water is bubbling slowly and whisk in the eight egg yolks one at a time. Continue whisking over the simmering water until the mixture thickens like a lemon curd. Remove the top half of

the double boiler or the bowl from the heat and whisk 1 minute at room temperature. Set the bowl aside to cool for 10 minutes, whisking occasionally.

3. Place the five egg whites and salt in a large bowl and beat with an electric mixer at high speed until soft, airy peaks form. Set aside.

4. Clean the mixer's beaters and beat the cream in a second bowl until doubled in volume but not stiff and buttery.

5. Fold the beaten egg whites into the lemon mixture, then gently fold in the whipped cream. Pour this mixture into the prepared soufflé dish; gently smooth the top with a rubber spatula.

6. Place the soufflé in your freezer and chill until set, at least 6 hours, or overnight. Once firm, cover the frozen soufflé with plastic wrap to guard against freezer odors; the soufflé can be stored in the freezer for up to 2 weeks. To serve, peel away the wax paper or parchment collar and let stand at room temperature for 5 minutes. Scoop out servings with a large spoon and top with the Fresh Berry Sauce (page 221).

NOTE: You can substitute 2 cups purchased nondairy whipped topping for the whipped cream. Omit step 4.

Customize it!
You can substitute any of the following in equivalent amounts for the lemon juice and zest: grapefruit juice and finely grated grapefruit zest, lime juice and finely grated lime zest, or orange juice and finely grated orange zest.

Fresh Berry Sauce

Here's a simple way to serve this luscious soufflé: just spoon it out onto a little of this fresh, summery sauce.

1 pint fresh raspberries, blackberries, or hulled strawberries
2 tablespoons sugar
1 tablespoon lemon juice

Place the berries, sugar, and lemon juice in a blender, food processor, or mini food processor; blend or pulse until pureed. If desired, strain through a fine-mesh sieve before serving. Store, tightly covered, in the refrigerator for up to 1 week.

Frozen Strawberry Bavarian Cream Cake

Makes 10 servings

This flavorful frozen cake is like a frozen mousse cake, only denser: a strawberry-infused Bavarian cream, placed in a gingersnap crust.

45 gingersnap cookies
¼ cup plus 3 tablespoons sugar
6 tablespoons unsalted butter, melted and cooled
1½ pints fresh strawberries (about 3 cups), hulled and cut into quarters, or two 10-ounce bags frozen strawberries, thawed
One ¼-ounce package unflavored gelatin
1 cup whole milk
8 large egg yolks, at room temperature
¾ cup cold heavy cream
4 large egg whites, preferably from pasteurized eggs, at room temperature
¼ teaspoon salt

1. To make the crust, crumble the cookies in a large food processor fitted with the chopping blade, add 3 tablespoons sugar, and process until finely ground. With the machine running, pour the melted butter through the feed tube; continue processing just until the mixture begins to gather together—all the crumbs should be uniformly moist. Pour half this crumb mixture into a 9-inch springform pan; press it gently but evenly across the bottom. Pour the remainder around the inner seal of the pan; press this amount up the side walls about 1½ inches, taking care also to even out the bottom crust. Set the pan in the freezer while you make the filling.

2. Puree the strawberries in a large blender until smooth. Pour in a medium bowl and stir in the gelatin. Set aside at room temperature for 10 minutes.

3. Meanwhile, heat the milk in a medium saucepan set over medium heat until small bubbles pop up along the pan's inner rim. Reduce the heat so the milk does not boil while you beat the egg yolks.

4. To make the custard, beat the egg yolks and the remaining ¼ cup sugar in a medium bowl with an electric mixer at medium speed until the mixture makes satiny ribbons that fall off the beaters when they're stopped and pulled up, about 4 minutes. Beat in about half the hot milk at low speed, then beat or whisk this combined mixture into the remaining hot milk in the pan. Immediately reduce the heat to low—if you're working on an electric stove, move the pan to a second burner just now turned to low—and cook, stirring constantly, until thick enough to coat the back of a wooden spoon, about 4 minutes.

5. Remove the pan from the heat and stir in the berry mixture. Continue stirring for 1 minute to cool the mixture a bit and dissolve the gelatin. Strain through a fine-mesh sieve into a second bowl. Refrigerate until slightly thickened, about 1 hour. (You can speed up the process by placing the bowl in an ice-water bath and stirring constantly with a rubber spatula until the mixture is slightly thickened, about 4 minutes.)

6. Meanwhile, clean and dry the mixer's beaters. Beat the cream in another medium bowl until doubled in volume but still creamy, not stiff or buttery. Set aside.

7. Clean and dry the beaters again. Beat the egg whites and salt in yet another bowl until soft, droopy peaks form when you turn off the beaters and lift them out of the mixture.

8. Now assemble the Bavarian cream. Use a rubber spatula to fold the beaten egg whites into the chilled strawberry mixture. Then gently fold in the whipped cream, just until no white streaks are visible. Pour into the prepared springform pan, taking care not to dislodge the crust. Smooth the top, then chill in the freezer until firm, for at least 4 hours or overnight. When the cake's firm, cover the pan with plastic wrap; the frozen cake can be stored this way for up to 1 week, although it will taste best within 48 hours of its being made.

9. To serve, remove the plastic wrap. Run hot water over a thin knife, wipe it dry, then run it around the inside of the cake pan, between the crust and the pan, loosening the cake's crust from the pan's sides without nicking the pan. Unlatch the

pan and remove the collar-like ring. Place the cake on a serving platter and slice into wedges as desired.

Frozen Blackberry Bavarian Cream Cake   Substitute blackberries for the strawberries.

Frozen Raspberry Bavarian Cream Cake   Substitute raspberries for the strawberries.

Frozen Tiramisù

Makes 6 servings

Tiramisù means "carry me up" in Italian—some assume "to heaven." A frozen version of this classic ladyfinger-coffee-cream-and-shaved chocolate dessert is sure to offer some sort of Paradise on a hot day.

> 30 purchased ladyfinger cookies
> 4 large egg yolks, at room temperature
> ¾ cup sugar
> ¼ cup brandy or dry Marsala
> 8 ounces mascarpone cheese
> 2 large egg whites, at room temperature
> ¼ teaspoon salt
> ⅛ teaspoon cream of tartar
> ½ cup cold heavy cream
> 2 teaspoons instant espresso powder
> 2 ounces semisweet chocolate, shaved with a vegetable peeler
>   or a microplane

1. Line a 9 x 5-inch loaf pan with plastic wrap, pressing it into the corners and leaving enough overlap so that the pan can later be sealed tightly. Line all sides of the pan with standing-up ladyfingers, turning the rounded sides out (save the remainder of the cookies for the top, later in the recipe). Place in the freezer while you prepare the custard.

2. To make the custard, bring about 2 inches of water to a boil in a medium saucepan; reduce the heat so the water simmers gently. Place the egg yolks and ¼ cup sugar in a bowl that will fit snugly over the pan; beat with an electric mixer at medium speed away from the heat until foamy and thick, about 1 minute. Beat in the brandy or Marsala, then place the bowl over the simmering water and continue beating at medium speed until mayonnaise-like, about 2 minutes.

3. Remove the bowl from over the pan (keep the water boiling) and beat in the mascarpone until smooth, scraping down the sides of the bowl as necessary. Set aside at room temperature.

4. Now make the cooked meringue that will lighten the custard. First, clean and dry the mixer's beaters. Place the egg whites, salt, and the remaining ½ cup sugar in a second bowl that will also fit over the saucepan; beat at medium speed away from the heat until foamy. Add the cream of tartar, place the bowl over the heat, and beat at high speed until smooth, thick, and shiny, scraping down the sides of the bowl with a clean rubber spatula as necessary, about 3 minutes. Remove from the heat and continue beating until room temperature, about 1 minute. Fold the cooked meringue into the custard and set aside.

5. Clean and dry the mixer's beaters again. Beat the cream and instant espresso powder in yet another bowl until the mixture has doubled in volume and will hold its shape when mounded. Gently fold into the custard mixture, taking care not to deflate the whipped cream but incorporating it fully. Fold in the shaved chocolate, then pour into the prepared loaf pan, taking care not to dislodge the ladyfingers on the sides. Smooth the top and cover with the remaining ladyfingers, flat side up. Return to the freezer and chill until set, for at least 4 hours or overnight. Once it's cold, fold the excess plastic wrap up over the top of the pan to seal it tightly; the frozen tiramisù can be stored this way for up to 2 weeks, although it will taste best within 48 hours of its being made.

6. To serve, peel the plastic wrap away from the top and turn the loaf pan upside down on a serving platter. Let stand for 5 minutes, then rock the pan back and forth, holding the plastic wrap against the platter, until the loaf pan comes loose. Remove the pan and all plastic wrap. Slice as you would a loaf of bread and serve with a fork.

Frozen Tropical Pie

Makes 8 servings

This creamy coconut and pineapple pie is like an island fantasy: a cool breeze on a hot day. Use coconut milk, regular or low-fat, but not cream of coconut, best for a tropical drink to accompany this frozen treat.

35 vanilla wafer cookies

¾ cup plus 2 tablespoons (14 tablespoons) sugar

5 tablespoons unsalted butter, melted and cooled

One 20-ounce can crushed pineapple in juice (not syrup), drained, liquid reserved

Two ¼-ounce packages unflavored gelatin

One 5½-ounce can unsweetened coconut milk

2 large egg whites, at room temperature

¼ teaspoon salt

⅔ cup cold heavy cream

⅓ cup shredded sweetened coconut

1. To make the crust, crumble the wafer cookies in a food processor fitted with the chopping blade, add the 2 tablespoons sugar, and process until finely ground. With the machine running, pour in the melted butter through the feed tube; continue processing just until moistened and uniform. Pour into a 9-inch pie plate and press across the bottom and up the sides to form an even crust, all the way up until it's level with the rim of the pie plate. Place in the freezer while you prepare the filling.

2. Place the reserved liquid from the crushed pineapple in a small bowl, sprinkle the gelatin over it, and set aside to soften at room temperature for 5 minutes.

3. Meanwhile, heat the coconut milk in a medium saucepan set over medium heat until barely simmering. Remove the pan from the heat and stir in the gelatin mixture until dissolved. Cool for 5 minutes, then mix in the crushed pineapple. Trans-

fer to a large bowl and place in the refrigerator until the mixture starts to set, about 25 minutes.

4. Now prepare the cooked meringue that will give the filling its marshmallowy texture. Bring about 2 inches water to a simmer in a medium saucepan set over high heat; reduce the heat so the water's simmering gently. Place the egg whites, remaining ¾ cup sugar, and salt in a medium bowl that will fit snugly over the pan; beat away from the heat with an electric mixer at medium speed until foamy. Place the bowl over the saucepan and continue beating at medium speed, scraping down the bowl with a rubber spatula, until shiny, smooth, and thick, about 3 minutes. Remove the bowl from the heat—be careful of escaping steam which can burn your fingers—and continue beating until room temperature, about 1 minute.

5. Use a rubber spatula to fold this cooked meringue into the cool, thickening pineapple mixture. Return the bowl to the refrigerator for 15 minutes.

6. Clean and dry your mixer's beaters. Beat the cream in a medium bowl until doubled in volume and firm, but not yet dry and buttery. Fold into the pineapple mixture until no white streaks are visible, then mound into the prepared pie shell. Freeze until firm, for at least 4 hours or overnight.

7. While the pie is setting up, preheat the oven to 325°F. Spread the coconut on a large baking sheet and bake, stirring frequently, until lightly browned, about 4 minutes. Pour into a small bowl and cool completely.

8. Once the pie's firm, sprinkle the coconut over the top and cover it with plastic wrap; the pie can be stored this way for up to 2 weeks. To serve, remove the plastic wrap, let the pie stand at room temperature for 5 minutes, and slice as desired.

Ice Cream Sandwiches

Makes 12 sandwiches

Chiffons, mousses, pies—they're all good, no doubt. But does anything really bring on the smiles like a platter of ice cream sandwiches? Especially made with big soft chocolate cookies and homemade gelato?

> 2¼ cups all-purpose flour
>
> ⅔ cup cocoa powder, sifted
>
> ½ teaspoon baking soda
>
> ½ teaspoon salt
>
> 12 tablespoons (1½ sticks) unsalted butter
>
> ¼ cup solid vegetable shortening
>
> 1⅓ cups sugar
>
> 1 large egg, at room temperature
>
> 1 tablespoon vanilla extract
>
> 1 quart gelato of any flavor, softened—try Vanilla (page 98), Chocolate (page 30), Espresso (page 44), Honey (page 55), or Peanut Butter (page 75)

1. Position a rack in the center of the oven and preheat the oven to 350°F. Whisk the flour, cocoa powder, baking soda, and salt in a medium bowl until uniformly colored; set aside as well.

2. Cut the butter into small pieces and drop them in a large bowl. Let stand for 2 minutes, then add the shortening and beat with an electric mixer at medium speed until creamy, about 1 minute. Add the sugar and continue beating at medium speed until light and smooth, about 2 minutes. Beat in the egg, then the vanilla. Remove the beaters and stir in the prepared flour mixture with a rubber spatula, just until moistened.

3. Sprinkle a few drops of water on your work surface and lay a large sheet of wax paper across it (the water will help it stay in one place). Divide the dough in half. Place half on the wax paper, cover with a second sheet of wax paper, and roll into

a rectangle about ¼ inch thick. Transfer this whole packet (wax paper/dough/wax paper) to a large baking sheet and chill in the refrigerator for 15 minutes. Repeat with the other half of the dough, two more sheets of wax paper, and a second baking sheet.

4. Slip the wax paper–covered sheets of dough off the baking sheets and onto your work surface. Line both the baking sheets with parchment paper or a silicone baking mat; return them to the refrigerator while you cut out the cookies.

5. Cut the dough into twenty-four 4-inch circles, using a large round cookie cutter or a thick-lipped drinking glass with an opening of a similar diameter (a thin-lipped glass will break). Remove the excess dough, then transfer the cookie rounds to the cold baking sheet with a metal spatula. Prick each cookie several times with a fork, creating a decorative pattern across the top, if desired.

6. Return one of the sheets to the refrigerator and bake the other until the cookies are dry to the touch, 13 to 15 minutes. Cool on the sheet for 3 minutes, then transfer to a wire rack with a metal spatula. Bake and cool the other sheet of cookies. Cool the cookies completely before making the sandwiches.

7. Spread twelve of the cookies with about ⅓ cup gelato, using an offset icing spatula or a small rubber spatula. Top each with a second cookie, thereby making 12 sandwiches. Place them on a large baking sheet and freeze in the freezer for about 2 hours. Wrap each sandwich in plastic wrap and store in the freezer for up to 2 weeks.

A No-Cook Version   One very easy way to make ice cream sandwiches is to buy 24 large, 4-inch round cookies, often the kind packaged separately. Buy 3 pints of premium ice cream and place it in the freezer until hard, about 4 hours. Place one container on its side on your work surface; using a serrated knife, slice down through the container, making four perfect rounds of ice cream. Peel off the carton and place one round on a cookie; top with a second. Repeat, making 12 ice cream sandwiches with 12 ice cream disks sliced from the containers. Freeze on a large baking sheet until firm, then wrap individually in plastic wrap for storage in the freezer.

ICE CREAM TERRINE

Makes 6 servings

Aproper ice cream terrine is all about the bright colors and intense, layered flavors. If you use the gelato recipes in this book, you'll need either to halve them to make 1 pint each or use half the gelato made in a full recipe.

> One 10- to 12-ounce purchased pound cake
> 1 pint Raspberry Gelato (page 88), or 1 pint purchased raspberry ice cream, softened
> ¼ cup coconut rum
> 1 pint Banana Gelato (page 18), or 1 pint purchased banana ice cream, softened
> 1 pint Mint Gelato (page 67), or 1 pint purchased mint ice cream, softened

1. Line a 9 × 5-inch loaf pan with plastic wrap, pressing it into the corners but with enough excess that the wrap can later be closed over the top to seal the pan. Place the cake on a cutting board and slice it horizontally into at least six ¼-inch-thick pieces using a long, thin knife. Lay one of the cake slices in the prepared loaf pan, cutting it to fit. Use two more slices of cake to cover the inside walls of the loaf pan, cutting them to fit and creating a pound-cake shell for the terrine.

2. Spread the raspberry gelato or ice cream into the terrine, taking care not to dislodge the pound cake. Smooth with a rubber spatula, then top with another slice of pound cake cut to fit the pan. Sprinkle this piece of pound cake with 2 tablespoons of the coconut rum.

3. Spread and smooth the banana gelato or ice cream into the terrine, then top with another layer of pound cake that's been cut to fit. Sprinkle this cake layer with the remaining 2 tablespoons coconut rum. Spread and smooth the mint gelato or ice cream into the terrine. Top with a final layer of pound cake. Seal the terrine tightly with the excess plastic wrap; place it in the freezer for at least 4 hours or overnight.

4. To serve, peel back the plastic wrap that covers the top of the terrine and turn the loaf pan upside down on a cutting board or serving platter. Moisten a few paper towels with hot water, then wring them dry and wipe the outside of the pan. Rock the pan back and forth, holding down the plastic wrap, to release the terrine. Remove the pan and all plastic wrap. Slice as you would a loaf of bread—a serrated knife works best.

Customize it!

Customize this terrine by using any gelato or sherbet combination in this book, or any purchased ice creams, sherbets, or sorbets. Match the colors and tastes to fit the season, holiday, or your own preferences.

ICE CREAM TRUFFLES

Makes about 40 truffles

Here's an easy treat for your get-together: little ice cream balls, covered in chocolate, like frozen candy bars. The secret to perfect frozen truffles is a small ice cream scooper, one that will make 1-inch balls. Look for one at baking-supply or candy-supply stores.

> 1 pint Vanilla Gelato (page 98), frozen hard, or 1 pint purchased premium vanilla ice cream
> 24 chocolate cream sandwich cookies, such as Oreos, finely ground in a food processor and spread on a plate
> 40 toothpicks
> 16 ounces (1 pound) semisweet chocolate, chopped
> 2 tablespoons unsalted butter, cut into chunks

1. Cover a baking sheet with wax paper. Scoop out a ball of the hard gelato or ice cream with a 1-inch ice cream scoop. Or use a sturdy tablespoon measure, scoop up a heaping bit of gelato or ice cream, and form this quickly into a ball. In either case, work quickly and roll the ball in the crumbled cookies to coat it. Place on the prepared baking sheet and repeat, making about 40 balls. Stick a toothpick in each ball. Place in the freezer until hard, about 3 hours.

2. Place about 1 inch water in the bottom half of a double boiler or in a medium saucepan and bring to a boil over high heat. Reduce the heat so the water simmers gently. Place the chocolate in the top half of the double boiler or a bowl that fits securely over the pan. Stir constantly until half the chocolate has melted. Be careful of any escaping steam—not only can it burn your hands, it can also condense in the chocolate and turn it to threads, thereby rendering it fairly useless for this recipe (see Note). Remove the pan from the heat, add the butter, and continue stirring until smooth. Set aside to cool for 15 minutes.

3. Take the baking sheet with the balls out of the freezer. Using the toothpick as a holder, dip each ice cream ball in the chocolate. Dip quickly, just to coat. Shake off any excess and return the ball to the wax paper–covered sheet. Remove the toothpick. Repeat with the remaining balls, removing the toothpick each time. Return the baking sheet to the freezer and freeze until hard, about 1 hour. When the balls are frozen hard, you can place them all in a large container, seal it well, and store them in the freezer for up to 2 weeks.

NOTE: When exposed to water vapor, melting chocolate can "seize"—i.e., the fat and solids can recombine into a stringy, gooey mess that's no good for coating desserts like this. You can try to save the mess by beating in heavy cream in 1 tablespoon increments, hoping the chocolate will re-adhere—but you have to hope for the best.

Customize it!
Substitute any cream-filled sandwich cookie for the chocolate cream sandwich cookies, such as peanut butter–cream sandwich cookies or vanilla-cream sandwich cookies or even strawberry sugar wafer cookies.

Substitute milk or white chocolate for the semisweet chocolate.

And/or substitute Chocolate Gelato (page 30), Espresso Gelato (page 44), Hazelnut Gelato (page 52), Pecan Gelato (page 77), or Walnut Gelato (page 100) for the Vanilla Gelato.

SPUMONI

Makes 6 servings

This classic frozen terrine has become a staple of Italian restaurants. Still, it's never as good as when you make your own gelato and fill the molded dessert with fresh whipped cream spiked with candied fruit.

> **1 quart Chocolate Gelato (page 30), or 1 quart purchased chocolate ice cream**
>
> **1 pint Pistachio Gelato (page 82, half the recipe), or 1 pint purchased pistachio ice cream**
>
> **¾ cup cold heavy cream**
>
> **3 tablespoons confectioners' (or "powdered") sugar**
>
> **¼ cup chopped glacéed cherries**

1. Line a 9 × 5–inch loaf pan with plastic wrap, pushing it into the pan's corners but also leaving enough excess over the sides that it can later be folded across the top to seal the pan.

2. Soften the chocolate gelato or ice cream by placing it in a large bowl and mashing it with the back of a wooden spoon, just until spreadable. Spread this softened gelato or ice cream into the prepared loaf pan, covering the bottom and sides evenly but leaving a wide trough in the middle of the pan. Place the pan in the freezer to chill for 1 hour.

3. Use the same technique as in step 2 to soften the pistachio gelato or ice cream. Again, spoon it into the loaf pan and use a rubber spatula to smooth it across the bottom and sides, making an even coating but leaving a hole in the middle of the terrine. Put the pan back in the freezer.

4. Beat the cream and sugar in a medium bowl with an electric mixer at high speed until firm but not yet dry and buttery. Fold in the glacéed cherries. Spoon this cream into the space still open in the loaf pan, smoothing it across the top to cre-

ate a layer of white that encases the terrine. Seal with the excess plastic wrap and freeze for at least 4 hours or overnight. The spumoni will stay this way for up to 2 weeks.

5. To serve, peel back the plastic wrap and turn the loaf pan upside down on a serving platter or cutting board. Wipe the pan with paper towels soaked with hot water and wrung fairly dry (so as to have hot towels without the water that could make the terrine soggy). Gently lift off the loaf pan; remove all plastic wrap. Slice with a serrated knife as you would a loaf of bread; serve on a plate with a fork.

Sundae Cones

Makes 12 sundae cones

Who didn't love these ice cream–truck favorites as a kid? With your own gelato, you might find your kids never even notice when the truck passes by.

> 12 mini marshmallows
> 12 conical sugar ice cream cones
> 1 quart Vanilla Gelato (page 98), or purchased vanilla ice cream
> ¼ cup purchased hot fudge sauce, warmed just until it's spreadable but not hot
> ¼ cup purchased caramel sauce
> ½ cup candy sprinkles, spread on a plate

1. Push a mini marshmallow into the bottom of each cone, so that it won't leak later as the gelato or ice cream melts.

2. Place about 1 tablespoon gelato or ice cream in a cone, pushing it down to the bottom. Drizzle in 1 teaspoon hot fudge sauce.

3. Place a slightly larger scoop of gelato or ice cream (about 1½ tablespoons) in the cone. Drizzle in 1 teaspoon caramel sauce.

4. Top the cone with an even larger scoop of gelato or ice cream, about 2 tablespoons. The ice cream can mound out of the top of the cone a little—round it off to a dome.

5. Dip the top of the cone in the sprinkles, then wrap it in plastic wrap and place it in the freezer on a large baking sheet.

6. Repeat with the remaining cones, gelato or ice cream, and sauces, dipping each in sprinkles before wrapping each in plastic wrap. Freeze for at least 2 hours or for up to 2 weeks.

Customize it!

Make these cones with any flavor gelato or purchased ice cream—from adult tastes like Mascarpone Gelato (page 65) or Pine Nut Gelato (page 80) to kid-friendly favorites like Chocolate Gelato (page 30) or Strawberry Gelato (page 94). You can also change the purchased ice cream toppings to any you think fit with the gelati or ice creams you've chosen.

TORTONI

Makes 12 individual tortoni

This classic Italian dessert is firmer than a semifreddo—closer to ice cream than that other marshmallowy treat.

> **12 paper muffin cups**
> **One 7–ounce bag sweetened shredded coconut (3 cups)**
> **2 cups cold heavy cream**
> **½ cup confectioners' (or "powdered") sugar**
> **½ teaspoon almond extract**
> **½ teaspoon vanilla extract**
> **¼ teaspoon salt**
> **2 large egg whites, preferably from pasteurized eggs, at room temperature**
> **6 maraschino cherries, cut in half**

1. Position a rack in the center of the oven and preheat the oven to 325°F. Line a 12-indention muffin tin with paper cups and set aside.

2. Spread 2 cups of the coconut on a large baking sheet; toast in the oven, stirring occasionally, until lightly browned, about 6 minutes. Set aside.

3. Beat the cream and ¼ cup of the confectioners' sugar in a large bowl with an electric mixer at high speed until soft peaks form when the beaters are turned off and lifted out of the mixture. Beat in the almond and vanilla extracts as well as the salt. Set aside.

4. Clean and dry the mixer's beaters. Beat the egg whites and the remaining ¼ cup confectioners' sugar in a large bowl until soft peaks form. Using a rubber spatula, fold about half the beaten cream mixture into the egg whites until fairly smooth, then fold in the remaining cream mixture and the remaining untoasted coconut. Use large, even arcs to fold the cream in—you want to incorporate it without deflating the mixture.

5. Spoon the mixture evenly into the prepared muffin cups. Divide the toasted coconut evenly among the tins, topping each one so it looks like a little haystack but gently pressing down so that the coconut adheres. Place half a cherry on top of each. Place in the freezer, preferably on the floor, until firm, at least for 4 hours or overnight. Once the tortoni are set, loosely cover the muffin tin with plastic wrap to protect against freezer odors. The tortoni may be stored this way for up to 2 weeks. Allow them to soften at room temperature for 5 minutes before serving.

Frozen Tortoni Soufflé   Omit the paper muffin cups and spoon the beaten mixture into a 1½-quart soufflé dish. Mound the top with the coconut and decorate with the cherries. Freeze as directed.

Customize it!
Stir in ¾ cup of the following with the vanilla: chopped hazelnuts, mini chocolate chips, shaved bittersweet or semisweet chocolate, or sliced almonds.

Source Guide

Buonitalia
75 Ninth Avenue, New York, NY 10011
212-633-9090
www.buonitalia.com
A wide range of Italian products, syrups, and flavorings, as well as packages of freeze-dried toasted peeled hazelnuts, a boon to any cook.

Kalustyan's
855 Rahway Avenue, Union, NJ 07083
908-688-6111
www.kalustyan.com
Passion fruit concentrate and a wide-ranging set of international condiments.

Marshall's Farm at The Flying Bee Ranch Honeytown
159 Lombard Road, American Canyon, CA 94503
800-624-4637
www.marshallshoney.com
Superior honey of all varieties from apiaries in Northern California.

Penzeys Spices
Stores across the Midwest and in Florida
P. O. Box 924, Brookfield, WI 53088
800-741-7787
www.penzeys.com
Dried spices and extracts, including high-quality vanilla extract.

Scharffen Berger Chocolate Maker
914 Heinz Avenue, Berkeley, CA 94710
800-930-4528
www.scharffenberger.com
A wide range of chocolates, nibs, cocoa, and specialty products.

Williams-Sonoma
Stores across the country
P. O. Box 7456, San Francisco, CA 94120
800-541-2233
ww5.williams-sonoma.com
Mixers, bowls, springform pans, and many flavorings and extracts.

www.ultimatecook.com
Recipes from and information on all nine Ultimate books, on Bruce and Mark, on our hard-cover book *Cooking for Two,* and a list of links to some of our favorite mail-order sources.

Index

Bavarian cream pie, frozen,
    184–86
    chocolate chip, 185
    coffee, 185
    orange, 186
    pineapple, 186
biscotti:
    espresso gelato, 45
    pistachio gelato, 83
blackberry(ies):
    in fresh berry sauce, 221
    frozen Bavarian cream cake,
        224
    gelato, 20–21
    sherbet, 130
black forest gelato, 27
blueberry:
    gelato, 22–23
    sherbet, 109
bombe, frozen, 187–89
    turning of, into baked Alaska,
        188–89
bourbon, in egg nog gelato, 42–43
brandy:
    Alexander pie, frozen, 199
    in cassata gelato, 24–25
    in frozen tiramisù, 225–26
brown sugar, pine nut gelato, 81
butter crunch banana gelato, 19

cakes, frozen, 180–240
    banana tofu cheesecake,
        182–83
    cheesecake, 190–91
    cherry lime ricky chiffon,
        192–93
    jelly roll, 200–201
    Key lime mousse, see Key Lime
        mousse cake, frozen
    layer, 204–6
    pans for, 181
    pineapple upside-down, see
        pineapple upside-down cake
    problems with, 180–81

raspberry chiffon, see raspberry
    chiffon cake, frozen
strawberry Bavarian cream, see
    strawberry Bavarian cream
    cake
timing preparation of, 181
candy sprinkles, in sundae cones,
    237–38
cantaloupe sherbet, 110–11
caramelized dulce de leche gelato,
    41
caramel sauce:
    in chocolate swirl gelato, 31
    in frozen Mississippi mud pie,
        207–8
    in pecan turtle gelato, 79
    in sundae cones, 237–38
caramel swirl, walnut gelato, 101
cashew, honey-roasted, dulce de
    leche gelato, 41
cashew brittle, in torroncino
    gelato variation, 97
cassata gelato, 24–25
champagne granita, 138
cheesecake:
    dulce de leche, gelato, 41
    frozen, 190–91
    lemon, gelato, 58
    orange, gelato, 72
"cheesecake," frozen banana tofu,
    182–83
cherries, glacéed:
    in Nesselrode semifreddo,
        168–69
    in spumoni, 235–36
cherry:
    gelato, 26–27
    granita, 139
cherry lime ricky chiffon cake,
    frozen, 192–93
chestnut(s):
    gelato, 28–29
    in Nesselrode semifreddo,
        168–69

chiffon cake, frozen:
    cherry lime ricky, 192–93
    peaches Melba, 216
    raspberry, see raspberry chiffon
        cake, frozen
    raspberry cream, 216
chocolate:
    almond, and fig gelato, 47
    almond swirl gelato, 9
    granita, 140
    macaroon, coconut gelato, 37
    in mocha gelato, 69–70
    mousse pie, frozen, 194–96
    raisin espresso gelato, 45
    "seizing" of, 234
    semifreddo, 161–62
    toffee espresso gelato, 45
chocolate, bittersweet, in
    stracciatella gelato, 92–93
chocolate, semisweet, in ice cream
    truffles, 233–34
chocolate, unsweetened, in bacio
    gelato, 15–17
chocolate chip(s):
    in almond candy bar gelato, 9
    in banana rocky road gelato,
        19
    Bavarian cream pie, 185
    coconut dulce de leche gelato,
        41
    in coconut gelato, 37
    in espresso chocolate raisin
        gelato, 45
    in espresso chocolate toffee
        gelato, 45
    in mendiant gelato, 14
    mint gelato, 68
    in orange chip gelato, 72
    in pecan turtle gelato, 79
    in pine nut chip gelato, 81
    in pistachio chip gelato, 83
    in pumpkin chip gelato, 85
    in walnut mocha chip gelato,
        102

chocolate cream sandwich
        cookies:
    in ice cream truffles, 233–34
    in Mississippi mud pie, frozen,
        207–8
chocolate fudge cookies, in black
        forest gelato, 27
chocolate gelato, 30–32
    in frozen bombe, 187–88
    in frozen Mississippi mud pie,
        207–8
    in ice cream sandwiches, 229–30
    rocky road, 31
    in spumoni, 235
    swirl, 31
chocolate ice cream:
    in frozen Mississippi mud pie,
        207–8
    in spumoni, 235
chocolate liqueur, in frozen
        chocolate mousse pie, 194–96
chocolate sandwich cookies, in
        frozen grasshopper pie,
        197–99
chocolate sauce:
    in almond chocolate swirl, 9
    in chocolate swirl gelato, 31
chocolate wafer cookies, in frozen
        raspberry chiffon cake,
        214–16
cinnamon gelato, 33–35
    apple pie, 34
    coffee cake, 34
    cookie-dough, 34
    crunch, 34
    date ginger, 34
    oatmeal cookie, 34
    raisin granola, 35
    walnut, 35
classic lemon sherbet, 117
coconut:
    chocolate chip dulce de leche
        gelato, 41
    gelato, 36–37

milk, in frozen tropical pie,
        227–28
    pecan orange gelato, 72
    rum lime gelato, 60
    sherbet, 112
coconut, shredded:
    in almond bar gelato, 9
    in frozen tropical pie, 227–28
    in mango rum gelato, 62
    in tortoni, 239–40
coffee:
    Bavarian cream pie, 185
    granita, 141
    hazelnut gelato, 53
coffee ice cream, in frozen
        Mississippi mud pie, 207–8
Concord grape granita, 142–43
cookie-dough cinnamon gelato, 34
Cosmopolitan granita, 148
cranberry:
    crunch ginger gelato, 51
    granita, 144
Crème de Banane liqueur, in
        coconut banana gelato, 37
crème de cacao, in orange chip
        gelato, 72
crème de menthe, in frozen
        grasshopper pie, 197–99

daiquiri:
    gelato, 60
    granita, 148
date, ginger cinnamon gelato,
        34
date gelato, 38–39
dulce de leche gelato, 40–41
    caramelized, 41
    cheesecake, 41
    coconut chocolate chip, 41
    honey-roasted cashew, 41
    truffle, 41

easy semifreddo, 163
egg nog gelato, 42–43

espresso gelato, 44–45
    biscotti, 45
    chocolate raisin, 45
    chocolate toffee, 45
    crunch, 45
    in frozen Mississippi mud pie,
        207–8
    fudge swirl, 45
    in ice cream sandwiches,
        229–30
    maple walnut, 45

fig gelato, 46–47
fior di crema, 48–49
fresh berry sauce, for frozen
        soufflé, 221
frozen desserts, 180–240
    as irresistible, 1
    pans for, 181
    problems with, 180–81
    product sources for, 241–42
    timing preparation of, 181
fudge:
    hazelnut gelato, 53
    nut banana gelato, 19
    sauce, see hot fudge sauce
fudge swirl:
    espresso gelato, 45
    mint gelato, 68
    walnut gelato, 101

gelato, 3–104
    air in, 4
    cream in, 3–4
    definition of, 3
    eggs in, 3, 4, 5
    mix-ins for, 7
    tips for successful, 5–6
    whole milk in, 3, 4
    see also specific gelati
gianduja gelato, 17
ginger:
    apple granita, 136
    date cinnamon gelato, 34

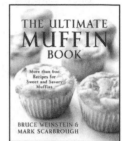
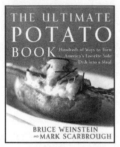
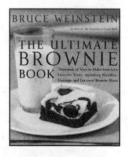
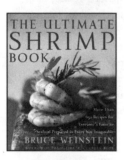
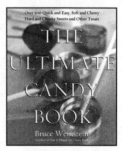

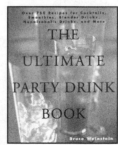